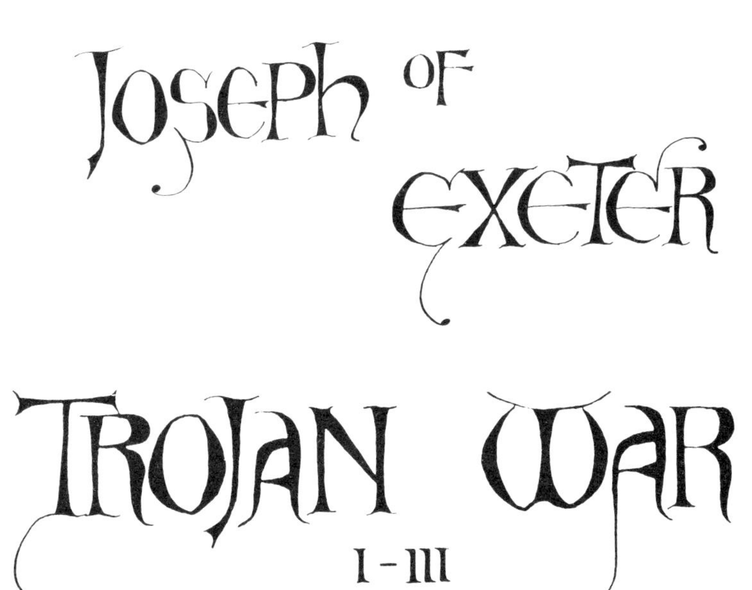

edited with translation and notes by

BOLCHAZY - CARDUCCI PUBLISHERS / ARIS & PHILLIPS LTD

British Library Cataloguing in Publication Data

Joseph, of Exeter
The Trojan war I - III. - (Classical texts)
I. Title II. Bate, A.K. III. Series
871'.03 PR2006.J6

ISBN 0 85668 294 2 *cloth*
ISBN 0 85668 295 0 *limp*

Printed and published in England by ARIS & PHILLIPS Ltd, Teddington House, Warminster, Wiltshire, England.

CONTENTS

PREFACE

When one thinks of medieval epic poetry one invariably recalls the famous examples to be found in the vernacular languages, *Beowulf, The Song of Roland, The Cid, The Nibelungenlied*. Latin epics rarely come to mind. Yet if it is true that some of the Latin epics are uninspired re-workings of vernacular texts, not all deserve to be rejected or forgotten. A work like the anonymous *Ruodlieb* is of great literary interest for its subject-matter and the attitude of its author towards the knight as hero in a changing society in eleventh-century Germany, despite its rather substandard versification or linguistic sophistication. In the twelfth century Alan of Lille adopted the epic form for his exposition of the Neo-Platonist philosophy being taught in France, while Walter of Châtillon and Joseph of Exeter reverted to the ancient world for their subject-matter. Yet they were not content to copy ancient epic poets they considered liars. Instead, they based their poems on writers they thought of as historians, such as Quintus Curtius or Dares Phrygius. Moreover, wittingly and sometimes unwittingly, they applied their own contemporary morality and ideas to the ancient material, creating a new blend. A further quality they possessed, that was unavailable to the mid eleventh-century *Ruodlieb* author, was a thorough grasp of the Latin language through the careful reading of an extremely large number of classical and post-classical authors. These authors were so well assimilated that their style and tone are found in their disciples, but not often their actual expressions. This easy familiarity with the *auctores* was the result of the excellent schools that flourished in northern France for most of the twelfth century, where the study of Latin literature received a huge stimulus, particularly from about 1125 to 1185, from the new evaluation of human worth subsequent to the publication of St. Anselm's *Cur Deus Homo*. In the case of Joseph, W.B. Sedgwick wrote 'Accordingly it is difficult to apportion his indebtedness. Perhaps he comes nearest to Statius in general treatment; in satirical passages he owes much to Claudian; on moral themes he often comes closest to Juvenal..; in his inexhaustible ingenuity he was an apt pupil of Ovid; in battle-pieces he chiefly uses Vergil and Statius. But his borrowings are usually too subtly interwoven with his own texture to be readily detached.' And even then Sedgwick somehow forgot to mention Lucan whom he considers to be one of the most important influences on Joseph - a fact that will be evident in the various mentions of Lucan in my Commentary.

Joseph was therefore able 'to stamp (his work) with his own individuality' (Sedgwick). We do not get the impression that he was merely writing in the Latin language; rather, that he was using Latin virtually as a mother tongue in the composition of an epic that has as much right to be read as any vernacular counterpart.

I should like to acknowledge my debt of gratitude to the various libraries that sent me microfilms of the Joseph manuscripts in their holdings or allowed me to read those MSS in situ: Cambridge Corpus Christi, Bodleian Oxford, Westminster Abbey, Admont Stiftsbibliothek, Paris Bibliothèque Nationale. My thanks are also due to colleagues at Reading, especially Dr J.G. Landels, for their willingness to discuss problems, and to Mrs Sybil Lowery for preparing this edition on the word-processor.

My greatest debt, however, is to Professor P.G. Walsh, whose careful reading of my typescript saved me from various slips and serious errors. I have adopted some of his suggestions for improving the work but on occasion have retained my own interpretation or that of Joseph's glossators against his views. Naturally, I bear responsibility for these decisions and any errors that ensue.

Reading 1985

INTRODUCTION

The Author

Joseph of Exeter is a fairly shadowy figure from the twelfth century despite his obvious abilities in the field of literature. Like many other poets and prose-writers of the period he has left us very few traces of his existence, even making the task of discovery harder by disseminating his epic on the Trojan war under the title of *Ylias Daretis Phrygii*. The few material facts that can be gleaned have to be sifted with care, as Ludwig Gompf has shown, for some of them prove to be quite modern in origin.[1]

That Joseph was the author of the epic is attested very soon after its composition. Before 1210, in his commentary on Alan of Lille's *Anticlaudianus*, William of Auxerre glosses the following lines

Illic pannoso plebescit carmine noster
Ennius et Priami fortunas intonat (1.165-66)

thus:

noster - quia Latinus poeta est noster, id est
contemporaneus, et significat Ioseph Cantuariensem;
Yliadum lacrimas etc.[2]

William is undoubtedly correct in his interpretation. Not only is *Yliadum lacrimas* the opening of the poem, but *plebescit* is probably a sarcastic reference to Joseph's frequent depiction of the *plebs* in his epic and to his use of the word at 6.348. It is to be noted that the place-name associated with him by William is Canterbury.

At the same period an Englishman, Gervase of Melkley, in his *Ars Poetica*, written between 1208 and 1216, quotes 4.. 175 of the poem with the attribution

Ioseph in Darete suo...inquit

The Cambridge MS of Joseph is preceded by a twelve-line elegiac poem in praise of the author of the epic that begins

Cresce, Ioseph, nomen augmenti moribus imple

playing on God's words to the Old Testament Jacob to go and increase (*Cresce* Genesis 35.11) and Jacob's words on his son, Joseph *accrescens* (49,22). In St. Jerome's *Liber de Nominibus Hebraicis* Joseph is glossed '*incrementum*'. As the date of the MS is late thirteenth century, long after Joseph's death, the author of the poem must have been a contemporary of Joseph since the epic itself gives no indication of Joseph's authorship.

Further evidence comes from the two glosses on the epic,

found in the Admont and Paris MSS.[3] The Admont glossator, who gives a more copious commentary than the Paris one, notes at 1.198

> *nostra* - quia Anglicus erat iste

and at 5.537

> *nobis* - scilicet Anglicis, quia Anglicus erat auctor iste et vocatus Ioseph.

At the end of the Commentary he writes

> Expliciunt glossule Frigii Darethis Yliados quem Magister Ioseph Anglicus composuit ad honorem Baldwini Cantuariensis Archiepiscopi.

In 1188 two Canterbury monks write of a Magister Ioseph with Baldwin at Reims en route for the Third Crusade.[4] The fact that they do not give him any further identification suggests that they thought of him as Ioseph Cantuariensis.

The name Joseph of Exeter, while possibly correct, has no early corroboration for its authenticity. It seems to have originated with the sixteenth-century antiquarian, Leland, who saw a fragment of a MS of Joseph's now lost epic, *Antiocheis*, at Abingdon, from which he learned that Joseph was born at Exeter.[5] We know that Joseph was the nephew of Baldwin of Exeter,[6] later Archbishop of Canterbury, the dedicatee of Joseph's Trojan War epic and the intended hero of the *Antiocheis*, so it is probably reasonable to think of him as Joseph of Exeter. The Canterbury name would then refer to his renown when working there, probably in some secretarial position associated with the Archbishop.[7]

Very few precisions are possible, either, concerning the details of Joseph's life. Our earliest clue must lie in Alan of Lille's slighting remarks on Joseph's Trojan War epic which he contemptuously lumped together with Walter of Châtillon's *Alexandreis*. Alan's *Anticlaudianus* was written about 1182 so it is reasonable to think that Alan is referring to two epics recently composed at Reims. We know that Walter's *Alexandreis* was written in the first years of the 1180's, so it is likely that Joseph's epic was written at the same period. He himself tells us, 1.15-23, that he wrote the epic as a young man, which probably means about the age of twenty as a student at Reims, so that would give a date of birth circa 1160.[8] In all probability his family was of humble origin since Gervase of Canterbury, the biographer of his uncle, says that Baldwin was born 'in Exonia ex infimo genere', and Joseph himself refers to his plebeian song (1.11). He presumably went to school at Exeter, though there is no evidence to support this view.[9] Most of his education appears to have been acquired at Reims. In a letter to his friend (and patron?), Guibert of Gembloux, written in 1189, Joseph says that he is studying again at Reims *more solito*, hoping to continue his reading of theology and canon law which he had had to interrupt previously, but complaining that he was short of money and books. It would appear from this that his Canterbury connections were not very lucrative.[10] In another letter to Guibert, written in 1190, he bemoans the fact that he is forced to go on the Third Crusade with his Lord Archbishop. Presumably the news of his intended role as verse chronicler of the Crusade, referred to by Giraldus (cf. note 6) in the spring of 1188, had taken a long time to reach him in Reims. The fact that he wrote the *Antiocheis* suggests that he actually went to Palestine, though he obviously did not stay very long. Baldwin's death in 1190 released Joseph from his crusading obligations, and it is unlikely that Joseph would have stayed on any longer than necessary, since he had already voiced his reservations about the weather, the food and the living conditions to Guibert.[11] In any case, a letter written to Joseph by Guibert after 1194 reveals him to be a schoolteacher at Jodoigne in Belgium, while trying to continue his religious studies.[12] Guibert's remarks that Joseph has left his country and his family (*de terra et de cognatione tua egressum*), indicates that he had returned to England after leaving Palestine. What happened to him after 1194 we simply do not know.

Works

a) Trojan War

Date

As we have seen, Joseph composed this epic in Reims in the first years of the 1180's, but it is obvious that he made changes and additions in the years that followed. The earliest addition appears to be the lines at the end of Book 5 referring to the death of the Young King Henry, son of Henry II.[13] They give the undoubted impression that they were written immediately after his death, with some patron in mind, and can therefore be confidently dated to the second half of 1183. Young King Henry died at Chinon on June 11th, 1183, but some time would be needed for the news to reach Joseph's entourage. The other obvious additions concern Baldwin. Joseph's dedication of the epic to his uncle, 1.30-59, was written when Baldwin was Archbishop of Canterbury as lines 31-32 and 35 plainly indicate, so they must have been added between 1185 and his death in 1190.[14] Towards the end of the dedication (57-59), Joseph refers to Baldwin's decision to go on the Crusade, which would suggest a date after the spring of 1188. However, as Joseph's letter to Guibert shows, Joseph was unaware of his uncle's decision until 1189 at the earliest. At the very end of the epic (6.961-67), Joseph again refers to the Crusade and his role as verse chronicler. It is Gompf's view that Joseph made all his additions to the text when he was in Reims in 1188-89,[15] but certain questions then suggest themselves. Why did Joseph wait six years after Young Henry's death to write his encomium? Why should Baldwin have been interested in Henry's death? As regards the lines on Baldwin himself, they give the impression that he has only very recently become Archbishop of Canterbury, as Canterbury is learning (*discit*) about its incumbent. The reference to Baldwin's re-affirmation of Canterbury's position of liberty vis-a-vis the king would not appear to be contemporaneous with his decision to leave Canterbury for the Holy Land. Furthermore, the glosses in the Paris and Admont MSS show evidence of variant readings, at times of whole lines (e.g. at 1.39), and the reference to the return of King Arthur (3.472-73) is explained by the Admont glossator but not by the Paris one. It is obviously dangerous to argue *ex silentio*, but the most likely explanation for the Paris glossator's silence is that the two lines in question did not figure in his text. My own view is that Joseph went on modifying his text from 1182 until 1189 at least, but was not in a position to incorporate his changes into each copy of his text.[16]

Title[17]

No satisfactory title for the work has been agreed. In modern times English scholars seem to have opted for *Bellum Trojanum* or *De Bello Trojano*, which are, in fact, sixteenth-century inventions. Contemporary or near-contemporary writings refer to the *Ylias Daretis Phrygii* or even *Dares*. Although *Ylias Daretis Phrygii* might be a more accurate title it is neither informative nor helpful, and leads to confusion. It has often been wrongly considered to be the same text as *Dares Phrygius Metricus*,[18] while G. Robert's translation of Joseph under the title *The Iliad of Dares Phrygius* seems to have caused an almost total ignorance of its existence among medievalists. Gompf's adoption of a shortened version of the title, *Ylias*, is reasonable, but the small gain in accuracy thus achieved does not appear to warrant our dropping the title by which the work is usually known.

Contents

The source material for Joseph's epic comes, as his title suggests, from the *De Excidio Troiae Historia* of Dares Phrygius, whose late antique 'historical' account of the destruction of Troy was very common reading in the Middle Ages.[19] To this basic material Joseph has made his own additions. For the return of the Greeks after the war he had recourse to the account of Dictys Cretensis; for the mythological touches he seems to have drawn on Ovid's *Metamorphoses*, a standard text book in medieval schools with accompanying glosses, Hyginus' *Fables*, the so-called Vatican Mythographers (I and II, and possibly III), the *Excidium Troie*, a text more or less contemporary with Dares that deals with the fall of Troy in purely mythological terms, and whatever he could find in Lucan, Statius and their commentators.[20] The evidence of Dictys is found naturally only in Book 6; that of the others pervades the whole work, but perhaps is most obvious in Book 2, where, of course, Dares provides precious few details about the Judgement of Paris!

Book 1 deals with the first destruction of Troy by Hercules and his followers in retaliation for the lack of hospitality shown by its king, Laomedon, to the Argonauts when they were on their way to Colchis to steal the Golden Fleece. Priam, who had been fighting in eastern Phrygia, thus escaped death, and on his return to Troy became its new king. He rebuilt the city larger than before.

Book 2 deals with the Trojans' plans for revenge or at least the return of Hesione, Priam's sister who had been abducted by the Greeks. Antenor went on an unsuccessful mission to the Greeks to obtain her release. Paris then recounted his dream about the three goddesses who came to him for his judgement on their beauty, and the promise of a successful foray into Greece made to him by Venus.

Book 3 contains the account of Paris' expedition to Greece and his abduction of Helen. The Greek preparations for war are described together with the drowning of Castor and Pollux, Helen's brothers, who had left Greece before the rest of the fleet in the hope of catching up with Paris and Helen on the seas.

Book 4 describes the Trojan auxiliary forces and the individual leading Greek and Trojan figures. Achilles' visit to the oracle to enquire about his future is followed by the sailing of the Greek fleet and Achilles' devastation of Mysia.

Book 5 recounts the beginning of the main war, the deaths of Proteselaus and Patroclus, the power-struggle among the Greeks, the fight between Paris and Menelaus and the death of Hector.

Book 6 describes the change in Greek leadership with the subsequent murder of Palamedes. Then follow the deaths of various warriors including Troilus, Memnon, Achilles, Paris, Ajax and Penthesilea. Troy is betrayed by the Antenor faction, Priam is murdered. Finally the Greeks sail home.

However, these brief resumés of the contents of each book, taken from the glosses, give an unbalanced view as they suggest that Joseph's work is essentially narrative. A full description of just one part of one book, as Sedgwick has shown,[21] presents a completely different picture. The first part of Book 1 looks as follows:

1-59	Proem and dedication
60-70	The invention of ships due to greed; greed scours the earth and flouts the elements
71-77	The Argonauts were the first sailors
78-90	The first attempts were on a modest scale
91-94	The crew hesitate
95-98	Why ask for trouble and invent new deaths?
98-101	Sea do your worst
102-116	But the sea-gods welcome new votaries
117-118	The Argonauts land at Sigeum (2 lines!)
119-123	Uproar at Troy
124-136	Why fight the favourites of the gods, O Trojans, doomed to destruction?
137-143	The fight begins
144-157	Nestor advises patience; speech
158-159	The Greeks sail to Colchis (2 lines!)
159-181	Description of harbour and landing
182-186	Why describe the plowing, the dragon, etc?
187-198	What a wicked conspiracy!
199-202	They return
203-213	What rejoicings!
214-223	But Pelias is angry
224-243	His speech: 'What are you about, O Gods?'
244-247	His dissimulation
248-266	Victors' feast containing a satire on luxury
267-270	Hercules cannot rejoice
271-298	His self-reproach (soliloquy)
299-305	Compared to bull
306-315	Remarks on Fama

In those 315 lines Sedgwick notes 59 lines of preface, 59 of satire, 44 of description, 120 of rhetoric and only 19 of narrative. As he states (p.59) 'The conduct of the story was the last thing he troubled about; in fact he seems like Lucan, mainly concerned to get away from the story and concentrate on speeches, descriptions, rhetorical outbursts and moral and theological disquisitions'.

Style

The *locus classicus* for a discussion of Joseph's style is Sedgwick's article to which I have frequently referred. It may be summarised as follows:[22]

Metre

Joseph's hexameter is so closely modelled on Silver Latin poets such as Lucan that he can hardly be distinguished from them, apart from his bold use of elision which recalls Vergil. This use of Vergilian techniques makes his hexameters somewhat less monotonous than Silver Latin poets, although his predilection for the Golden line can be tiresome. False quantity is extremely rare and is sometimes due to the fact that his only source for certain names was the prose-writer Dares. It must be remembered too, that Joseph may often have had access to corrupt texts, something which would excuse some of his shortcomings and which Sedgwick does not appear to envisage.

Grammar

His grammar is very good. He imitates and surpasses the bold constructions of Silver Latin but he rarely sins through ignorance. The few 'irregularities' (!) that Sedgwick notes often have classical authority but it must be remembered that Joseph was not a classical poet nor was he attempting to be one. Consequently we should not consider a medieval usage as an irregularity. Medieval writers were not striving to write perfect classical Latin, rather they were using the classics to extend their powers of expression. Possibly the most noteworthy features are Joseph's use of the future participle and of the gerundive as a future passive participle. In addition to Sedgwick's comments it is worth noting that the use of a supine after a verb to denote purpose is not a common feature of medieval writers.

Joseph's lack of restraint is particularly evident in the ingenuity of his use of every conceivable rhetorical device and contortion of speech. However, unlike his contemporaries, who often used this excess of verbal agility to cloak their incapacity to think, Joseph combines his exuberance of ideas with that of his eloquence. For example, in Book 4 he gives a physio-psychological description of Helen's interior, in Book 5 he gives a highly coloured description of the carnage at Troy, using a varied arsenal of verbal tricks, including transferred epithets, nouns used adjectivally, periphrasis, prosopopeia, paronomasia, alliteration, assonance, apostrophe, hendiadys, metonymy, synechdoche, irony, *sententiae*, catalogues, etc. All these elements are prescribed and exemplified in the various Arts of Poetry of the Middle Ages, but along with other poets like Walter of Châtillon, Hugh Primas and the Archpoet, Joseph shows that the highly respected teachers who wrote these manuals were very pedestrian in their output. The real poets did not simply fill their verses with these devices; they used them to write exciting poetry.

Text

Until Gompf's edition of 1970 all the previous editions had been based on Albanus Torinus' 1541 edition which used a now lost MS.[23] Later editors re-printed this text with few changes and even these were conjectures. Even Sedgwick in 1930 had to use the Delphin reprint of 1825 of Dresemius' 1620 edition, supplementing it with Jusserand's 1877 edition of the first book from the Paris MS and Miss E.G. Parker's answers to his queries concerning the Oxford MS. As the first editions were influenced by Renaissance scholarly thought, direct Christian references were deleted or modified, so their evidence is suspect. Furthermore, they may well show original readings which Joseph was later to discard as he revised his work with patrons in mind. Consequently a text of Joseph must be based on the surviving MSS in my view. In 1951 G. Riddehough did just this, but his text remained as an unpublished Harvard dissertation. He collated the five known MSS and the Paris Commentary, but was unaware of the larger Admont Commentary. Gompf's edition uses all the known evidence. My own edition is based on the same material as Gompf's. I have personally transcribed all five known MSS and both commentaries. The differences between Gompf and myself are minimal - the occasional preference for the reading of one MS over another (without any radical change of meaning) and some punctuation changes. Gompf seemed unaware of the existence of a sixth MS of the text. I myself have not seen it because its location is still secret, I believe. It is probably that seen by the fourteenth-century humanist, Coluccio Salutati.[24]

MSS[25]

A = Admont Stiftsbibliothek 128

Probably written c. 1250-60 in Salzburg, Austria. It contains the text of Joseph as well as the beginning of a commentary in the margins of the first page of the text and a full commentary later on. Most of the texts in the MS have a northern French connection: Serlo of Wilton's *De Contemptu Mundi*, Walter of Châtillon's *Alexandreis*, Matthew of Vendôme's *Tobias*, Petrus Pictor's *De Sacra Eucharistia*, etc. The commentary on Joseph also appears to conform to this pattern as the authors cited as authorities for certain statements or else as examples of similar usage include Theodulus, Walter of Châtillon, Remigius of Auxerre along with the more predictable Lucan, Statius, Ovid, Juvenal, Claudian, Sallust and Macrobius. Other, unnamed writers whose influence is visible include John of Salisbury and Adam of St Victor. Furthermore, as we saw earlier, the commentator knew the identity of Joseph and Baldwin. He also shows knowledge of stories of the ghost of Becket appearing to his unworthy successor. All this is consonant with the identification of a Frenchman from the Reims area or of an Englishman who fled to Reims with Becket and then stayed on. However the glosses were made from a text different to the one in the Admont MS as it often has variant readings and even lines not to be found in the Admont text. The text and the glosses represent Joseph's poem at two different stages of its development.

C = Cambridge, Corpus Christi College 406
Written at the end of the thirteenth century in France by a scribe who knew that Joseph was the author of the poem and copied the short laudatory elegiac poem in front of the text. As with A, the contents are largely northern French, including John of Hauville's *Architrenius*, Bernard Silvestris' *Megacosmus*, Alan of Lille's *Anticlaudianus*, Geoffrey of Vinsauf's *Poetria Nova* and Walter of Châtillon's *Alexandreis*. The text is among the most accurate of Joseph that is extant, with only a few lacunae.

L = London, Westminster Abbey 18
Written in the first half of the thirteenth century in northern France. It contains only Joseph's epic. This MS is the best example we have of Joseph's text, with no lacunae. It could almost be printed as it stands.[26]

O = Oxford, Bodleian, Digby 57
Written towards the middle of the thirteenth century, probably in Battle, Sussex. It contains three of the texts found in C, those of Joseph, Bernard Silvestris and Alan of Lille. Some of the lacunae of O are identical with those of C. It has one lacuna of significance, I, 5, for that line has no gloss in either the A or P commentaries. It cannot be the source of the glosses however, since it lacks, with C, 4. 19-20, which are glossed,

but a MS similar to O must have provided the basis for the glosses. It is not so reliable as L and C but better than A and P.

P = Paris, Bibliothèque Nationale, Lat. 15015
Written towards the end of the thirteenth century by a careless scribe, probably from dictation by the look of some of the mistakes which are more easily explained as aural rather than visual. It is incomplete, finishing at 5.82. The gloss or commentary that accompanies it, however, is of the whole work. It is very similar to the commentary in A, though less helpful, with reference to the same classical authors. It differs however, in its use of French vernacular to explain certain points of difficulty. At 2.255, to explain Juno's pretended slip of the tongue the glossator adduces the French expression 'Singe mes sire', while at 2.515 he glosses *spuria* with '"bastarde" in vulgari'. Slightly puzzling is the gloss at 1.489-90 where he says of a sort of gate that 'dicitur in vulgari "porta collaticia"', an expression that looks still suspiciously like Latin. Other French characteristics are the totally gratuitous remark about the mercenary nature of the schools of Orleans at 2.489 and the use of 'locum habere' to mean 'to take place' or 'to happen' (cf. French avoir lieu).

b) Religious Poems

Although it is traditional to think that Joseph was a poet with totally secular interests[27] scholars like Raby appear to have seen him as a committed Christian who regretted that 'he had wasted his youth on trifles'.[28] The truth is more nuanced. Joseph's youth does indeed appear to have been spent in the schools of Reims where his preferences lay in the ancient authors, to judge by his Trojan War epic, although he was ostensibly studying theology and canon law, as his letters reveal.[29] This attention to theological matters may have been occasioned by his family links with Baldwin, or else by his desire to find a place in the entourage of the king or of some important prelate, in which case knowledge of canon law would have been essential. These same letters reveal that he found it difficult to concentrate on this side of his studies. He asked Guibert to impose some sort of penance on him, and Guibert sent him some of his own prose writings on the life of St Martin of Tours and on the theme of virginity which Joseph was to set to verse. The resulting poems, to be found among Guibert's correspondence,[30] show a high degree of competence. This is not surprising in respect of the metrical elegiac couplets of the poems on virginity, but an unexpected addition to Joseph's reputation as a poet is his skill in writing rhythmic verse, for the Sequence on the life of St Martin is a well-written rhythmic poem with two-syllable rhyme. However, they do not show that Joseph had come to terms with the tensions in his life between the secular and the religious. Raby's statement that 'he was soon carried away by the crusading movement',[31] is disproved by the letter to Guibert in which Joseph expressed his fears as he was forced to follow Baldwin on the Crusade. Furthermore, in our last mention of him, in Guibert's letter written in 1194 or after, he appeared to be still in the process of studying theology while earning his living as a teacher - a fact that indicates that he had not solved his dilemma.

c) Antiocheis

Of Joseph's epic on the Crusades we have very little information. Even by the sixteenth century there was probably no full text extant as Leland was able to find only a few lines at Abingdon. Those concerning Joseph's birthplace, Exeter, he described, while those dealing with Brutus and King Arthur he transcribed. These were later copied by Camden.[32] The contents of the epic obviously included the third crusade with the deeds of Baldwin and King Richard I. If Antioch is a place name then the epic must have included the first crusade as well, for it was in this one that Antioch was captured. If this is the case then structurally it would have been similar to the Trojan War epic and similarities would exist between the two titles - Antiocheis and Ylias both being Greek place names. However, as Gompf points out,[33] the -eis ending is normally attached to a personal name, and he suggests that Antiochus is used as a symbol of antagonism to the faith, though he limits the identification to Saladin in the Third Crusade. In all probability we will never know the reason for Joseph's choice of title for this epic.

Raby and Bezzola also talk of other writings of Joseph, including a panegyric on King Henry II, a *Cyropaedia*, numerous epigrams and love poems,[34] but our only evidence for the possible existence of these works is a statement by Bale which it is safer to disregard than to believe, for it seems highly unlikely that he would have discovered substantial writings of Joseph whose existence was unknown to Leland[35]

Sources of the Trojan War Story in the Middle Ages

To generations brought up on Homer and Virgil the story of the Trojan War is that told by the two great epic writers, for their superior literary talents have conferred upon their versions of the war almost a historical authority effectively relegating other versions to the status of curiosities. Yet this was not always so. In the Middle Ages another, anti-Homeric, version of the events carried most weight, that which is often called the Dares-Dictys tradition, and it did not obtain its position by mere default. Virgil's *Aeneid* was widely available and constantly used by teachers to explain hexameter construction, to provide material for précis exercises or for set topics such as the death of Hector. Homer's version was known through the abridgement of Baebius Italicus, the *Ilias Latina*.[36] Much of the Homeric material was also to be found in various parts of Ovid's *Metamorphoses* and *Heroides*, in Statius' *Achilleid*, in mythological writers such as Fulgentius, Hyginus and the Vatican mythographers (or their predecessors).[37] But while these authors were used for individual details or events they never provided the whole story or influenced the main stream of Trojan legend. Although the Middle Ages were under the impression that the origins of their tradition of the story went back to the war itself, their mistaken belief was not a late invention for it seems to have started in ancient Greece. The anti-Homeric version of the events appears to have started in the 6th century BC with Stesichorus, and was adopted by Euripides, but it was the rationalisation by the 4th-c.BC philosopher Euhemerus which seems to have been most influential.[38]

In the first century AD Euhemerus' rationalisation techniques afforded a spurious authenticity to Greek forgeries which purported to be eye-witness accounts of the Trojan War. Sisyphus of Cos claimed to be the scribe of Teucer while Korinonos the Ilian was Palamedes' scribe.[39] But far more important for the West was Dictys of Crete's eye-witness account.[40] Dictys claimed to have been in the retinue of Idomeneus and to have kept a journal of the events of the war, supplementing his information by conversations with Odysseus, Neoptolemus and others. Thus he provided plausible evidence for events or discussions to which he could not personally have been a party. Dictys' text exists in a Latin version which a 4th-c. Lucius Septimius said he had translated from the Greek, faithfully as regards the first five books but greatly abridged as regards the last four. Despite much dismissal of Lucius' claims in the past, it is now obvious that he was telling the truth, for we possess fragments of the original Greek text in the Tebtunis and Oxyrhynchos papyri which corroborate his words.[41] For Dictys the war was caused by Paris' abduction of Helen. As a result of this insult to the Greeks, Palamedes, Odysseus and Menelaus go to Troy to lodge a formal complaint but arrive before Paris. Priam can obviously do nothing for the moment and the Greek envoys are given hospitality by Antenor while awaiting Paris' return. Paris finally arrives and persuades his family to let him keep Helen. The Trojan people rebel against the royal family and Paris' quelling of the revolt is so brutal that Antenor has to intervene to put an end to the slaughter. Paris then plots to kill the Greek envoys who escape because of Antenor's discovery of the plans and timely warning. They return home and prepare for war, a huge effort that requires nine years. For the actual fighting in the war Dictys is actually indebted to Homer for the substance if not the treatment. Chryses, the Trojan priest of Apollo, brings a plague on the Greek camp and can only be placated by the return of his daughter who is Agamemnon's slave. Agamemnon agrees to give up his slave but insists on taking one from Achilles. Achilles sulks in his tent but with little detriment to the Greek cause thanks to the prowess of the other Greek leaders, until Agamemnon offers a full apology. Meanwhile the Trojan allies are becoming disaffected. Achilles falls in love with Polyxena and when confronted with Hector's terms for a deal is ready to put pressure on the Greeks to withdraw in order to be able to marry her. However, Hector kills Patroclus and Achilles vows revenge, obtaining his opportunity when Hector escorts the Amazon reinforcements. He drags Hector's body around the plain. After funeral games are held for Patroclus Priam and Polyxena ransom Hector's body. Neither the Amazons nor the later reinforcements of Memnon's troops help the Trojan cause. Achilles is tricked by a letter from Priam offering marriage to Polyxena and is murdered by Paris and Deiphobus. Their brother Helenus is appalled by this deed and goes over to the Greek side. Achilles's son, Neoptolemus, arrives to take command of the Myrmidons. Paris is killed by Philoctetes, and as the war continues to go against the Trojans some of the nobles, led by Antenor and Aeneas, make plans to surrender Troy to the Greeks. In concert with the Greeks Antenor hands over the Palladium while Helenus advises the building of a wooden horse. After due compensation has been paid to the Greeks they sail off, leaving behind the wooden horse. The Trojans are so relieved to see the back of the Greeks that they demolish a part of their city wall to take the horse inside. That night Sinon guides the Greeks back to Troy where they massacre the sleeping Trojans except for the familes of Antenor and Aeneas. After the departure of the Greeks Aeneas unsuccessfully attempts to drive out Antenor and is himself forced into exile. The work ends with the abridged version of the homecoming of the Greek leaders.

Dictys' version of the story presents Antenor not as a traitor but as a man acting humanely and judiciously, preventing slaughter, attempting to bring the war to an end. Aeneas has a very minor role, even in the betrayal of the city. Hector is a very unsavoury character, starting battle before a truce has expired, capable of killing only those Greeks already wounded by some other Trojan. Achilles has underhand methods of fighting - that is when he actually does any, for his love for Briseis and Polyxena keeps him in his tent for lengthy periods. Odysseus is particularly nasty, being responsible for the deaths of Palamedes, Telamonian Ajax, Polyxena and Hecuba, while being ready to sacrifice Iphigenia. Dictys' heroes are Palamedes, Idomeneus, Meriones and Telamonian Ajax.

Dictys' account of the war, translated into Latin, probably inspired some enterprising author to forge a Trojan view of the events, and sometime between the 4th c. and the 7th c. came into existence the *Historia de Excidio Troiae* of Dares Phrygius who claimed to be a soldier in the Trojan army.[42] Dares starts with the voyage of the Argonauts which he sees as the ultimate source of the conflict. Laomedon, the Trojan king, refuses to allow the Argonauts to stop in his country to rest and take on fresh supplies. Hercules takes this dereliction of the duty of hospitality as an insult and he later returns to Troy with an army of Greeks, destroying the city and killing Laomedon and his family, except for Priam who was absent in eastern Phrygia at the time of the battle. Priam returns to Troy and rebuilds it. He sends Antenor to Greece to ask for Hesione's return but Antenor is badly received by the Greeks. On his return to Troy he advocates invasion of Greece. Paris asks permission to lead the expedition as he has divine encouragement given him in a dream and guaranteeing him success. He sails to Cythera and abducts Helen whom Priam seems to think of at times as a possible exchange for Hesione. However, the Greeks retaliate by collecting a fleet. A meeting between the Trojan priest Calchas and Achilles at the oracle at Delphi results in Calchas joining the Greeks. A sacrifice to Diana gets the fleet on its way from Aulis safely to Tenedos. Achilles plunders Mysia for food and leaves Telephus there to provide a continuing source of supplies. The war is waged with generous periods of truce to bury the dead (Dares' method of accounting for ten years). Hector kills

Protesilaus, Patroclus, Merion and thousands more. Generally the Trojans are led into battle by Hector, Aeneas and Troilus. Andromache dreams of Hector's future death and persuades Priam to keep him in Troy, but considerable Trojan losses force Hector back into the fray where he is killed by Achilles. A year later Achilles visits Hector's tomb, sees Polyxena and falls in love with her. Priam agrees to the marriage on condition that Achilles brings about a peace settlement. Achilles tries to undermine the morale of the Greek army and refuses to help in the fighting. In his absence the new Trojan leader, Troilus, creates such havoc among the Greeks that they consider abandoning the siege, despite Calchas' encouragement, and Achilles finally relents so far as to allow his Myrmidons to join the battle again. When they are cut down by Troilus Achilles is provoked into action and after being wounded by Troilus he finally gets the better of him and puts him to death. Hecuba, who has now seen both Hector and Troilus killed by Achilles, plots revenge. She writes a letter to Achilles in Priam's name to lure him to the temple of Apollo, where he is ambushed by Paris. Helenus has his body returned to the Greeks. Neoptolemus is sent for and in the ensuing battle Ajax and Paris kill each other. Penthesilea arrives with her Amazons to help the Trojans, wounds Neoptolemus, but is then killed by him. The Trojans now lose heart, and Antenor, Polydamas and Aeneas, who had unsuccessfully put forward peace proposals to Priam and the elders, decide to betray Troy in return for their own safety. Their trustworthiness is put to the test by the Greeks and then one night Antenor and Aeneas open the Scaean Gate (which has a horse's head carved on it) to let in the Greeks. After the massacre the Greeks honour their agreement with the traitors until they realise that no trace of Polyxena has been found. Because Aeneas was hiding her he is exiled while Neoptolemus slits her throat over the tomb of Achilles. The work ends with the estimation of the length of the war (10 years, 6 months, 12 days), the number of dead (866,000 Greeks, 676,000 Trojans), and the destinations of the survivors.

This version is more un-Homeric than Dictys' and as it is presented from a Trojan (i.e. Western) viewpoint it was more popular, since most Western European nations claimed to be descended from the Trojans.[43] The glorification of Troilus was to have a considerable influence on later writers while the depiction of Aeneas as a traitor appealed to the nations in the 12th c. who were unhappy with Rome's insistence on making church appointments when previously that had been a royal prerogative. Whether any Greek text lies behind it, as claimed in the prologue, is difficult to ascertain. Otmar Schissel von

Fleschenburg (*Dares-Studien*, Halle, 1908) has shown that the first ten chapters are based on a Latin version of the Argonauts story, but felt that chapters 12 to 43 might be based on a Greek original.[44] The Latin text is very bitty[45] and looks like an abridgement, but of a Greek or Latin original? Furthermore, was the fuller version available at any time after the epitome was made?[46] A clue may be gleaned from the insertion in the Fredegar Chronicle, though the writer was doubtlessly composing from memory (a very faulty one) and was particularly stupid as well,[47] so the use of this text as evidence is fraught with difficulties. However, Gaston Paris has put forward certain arguments to suggest that the 7th-c. writer had read or heard a fuller version of the Dares text. He knew about the River Simois and its geography, his version of Helen's rape is not that of Dares but is similar to that of ancient writers, the role of Palamedes is even more important than in Dares, he gives Neoptolemus' speech at the death of Polyxena: all of these are elements beyond the intellectual capacities he shows elsewhere in his account, which suggests that they were present in his source. Thus a fuller version of Dares no doubt did exist at some stage, but there is no evidence to show that any later writer had access to it. As for the language of the fuller version it would have to be Latin, but the existence of an earlier Greek version is as yet no closer to being demonstrated. Together with occasional details from Dictys, Dares was the source for Benoit de Ste Maure's *Roman de Troie*, the 12th-c. Irish *Togail Troi*, Joseph of Exeter, Albert of Stade's *Troilus*, Guido de Columnis' *Historia Destructionis Troie*, Chaucer and Gower.

The third text of great importance to the Middle Ages, about which very little has been written, is the anonymous *Excidium Troie*, like Dares probably dating from the 6th c. Like Dares and Dictys the text tells the story in straightforward chronological, causal terms, but unlike them it makes no pretence to historical truth. The author nowhere impinges on the text as he recounts the story in purely mythological terms. For him the cause of the war lay in the marriage of Peleus and Thetis to which Discord was not invited. She turned up however, and threw her golden apple among the guests. We then learn of the fateful dream of the pregnant Hecuba, of the birth and subsequent exposure of Paris, his upbringing as a herdsman. He liked to hold fights between bulls, crowning the winner. One day Mars appeared disguised as a bull, fought with and defeated Paris' favourite bull. Because Paris crowned Mars he earned such a reputation for impartiality that Jupiter chose him to judge the three goddesses to see who would get the apple. Afterwards Paris is re-united with his family in Troy, having defeated his brothers in athletic contests, and then sets off for Greece, disguised as a merchant, to seek Hesione. However, he meets Helen who asks him to abduct her. Menelaus and Agamemnon collect a fleet and sail to Troy, only to find on arrival that they are fated to lose unless they have Achilles. Nobody knows who Achilles is, but after due investigation the Greeks learn of his youth, how his mother had dipped him in the Styx to make him invulnerable, and how he had been educated by Chiron. They send Odysseus and Diomedes to Lycomedes' harem where Achilles is living, disguised as a girl, and trick him into revealing his identity. They go off with him to Troy but he refuses to fight because of the loss of Briseida. When Hector kills Patroclus Achilles joins the fight, killing Penthesilea and Memnon. With the help of the two Ajaxes he disposes of Hector. Priam recovers Hector's body by handing over Polyxena in exchange and then persuades her to discover Achilles' weak spot. In the temple Paris shoots Achilles in the heel with a poisoned arrow. Neoptolemus is brought from Lycomedes' palace and the Greeks build a wooden horse. Sinon tricks the Trojans into taking it into their city, lets out the soldiers hidden inside and signals to the Greek fleet. The Greeks return and sack the city. The author then continues with a paraphrase of the *Aeneid* before giving a potted version of the early history of Rome.

MSS of this work are extant throughout Europe,[48] where it was used as a school text, influencing writers of Latin like Joseph, Walter of Châtillon and Simon Aurea Capra. More important, however, was its influence on writers in the vernacular languages, for the 13th-c. Norwegian *Trojumanna Saga*, the 14th-c. Bulgarian *Trojanska Prica*, the 13th-c. German *Trojanerkrieg* by Konrad of Würtzburg and the anonymous *Trojaroman* in MS Vienna 2802, are all based on it.[49] The *Excidium Troie*, or a text very similar to it (e.g. the *Compendium Historiae Trojanae-Romanae*, ed. H. Simonsfeld in *Neues Archiv der Gesellschaft für altere deutsche Geschichtskunde*, 11 (1886), 239-51, might be an abridged version of it) lies behind the 14th-c. English *Seege of Troy* and *Story of England* by Robert Mannynge of Brunne, the 13th-c. Spanish *Libro de Alexandre, Estoria General* of Alfonso the Wise, and *Sumas de Historia Trojana*, the 14th-c. Italian *Istorietta Trojana* and *La Fiorita* of Armannino Giudice, as well as the 14th-c. German *Gottweiger Trojanerkrieg*. Like Dares and Dictys it is written in straightforward, very simple, Latin, it tells the story in chronological order, and it shows that Achilles did not defeat Hector in a fair fight – a very important factor for the

Middle Ages when Hector was considered the perfect knight and consequently virtually invincible - while its insistence on the Achilles-Polyxena love interest helped to 'liberate' Briseida/Criseida so that the famous love story of Troilus and Cressida could take form in the 12th c., coinciding with the start of courtly love practices and the rise of the Arthurian legends.

Latin Versions of the Trojan War Story, 11c.-13c.[50]

Although MSS of Dares, Dictys and *Excidium Troie* were copied in the period from the 9c. to the 11c., they appear to have had little effect on literary production. Full-scale epic writing in Latin was concerned with the more immediate past, getting down in a 'permanent' language the deeds of the Carolingian emperors, the Norman invasion of France, etc. It was only in the second half of the 11c. when improved economic conditions had facilitated the spread of schools and learning from monasteries to cathedrals that interest in the literature of the past as models for literary production began to bring forth fruit. One of the earliest glimpses is an oblique reference. Godfrey of Reims recounts around 1070 a dream he had in which Odo of Orleans is supposed to have appeared to him to recite to him his poem on the Trojan War. Godfrey paraphrases the poem for us, but its contents are too general to give any hints of Odo's sources. In a later poem, circa 1180, Godfrey wrote his own version of events concerning the war, and while Ovid and Virgil are obviously models for the mise-en-scène some of the substance, particularly the judgement of Paris, may well have derived from the *Excidium Troie*. Around the turn of the century appeared the anonymous poem *Pergama flere volo*, one of the most popular Trojan War poems to be written in the period. The early part of the 12c. saw the production of several short poems on the topic. Baudri of Bourgueil imitated Ovid's *Heroides* for his letter exchange between Paris and Helen. Peter of Saintes, tutor to King Henry II of England, Hugh Primas and Simon Aurea Capra all turned out poems on the theme between 1125 and 1160 while an anonymous poet versified the text of Dares from chapter 11 onwards around 1150. Stohlmann has argued that writers became more prolix as the century advanced, with the result that with the anonymous Dares versification (918 lines) and Simon Aurea Capra's third version (994 lines), we are talking of little epics. The great leap forward, if so it is to be described, came with a French poem, *Le Roman de Troie*, written in the 1160's, containing 33000 lines, dedicated to Alienor of

Aquitaine, wife of Henry II. The work highlights features appreciated by the courtly audience it was written for, namely the love affairs of Jason and Medea, of Achilles and Polyxena, as well as creating the tragic love triangle of Troilus-Cressida-Diomedes. Benoit's poem was so successful that in the 13c. French prose versions were made of it, and in 1287 Guido de Columnis used one of these as a basis for his Latin text which was to achieve tremendous popularity, for over 150 MSS of Guido's text are extant.[51] It would be tempting to think that Joseph was influenced by Benoit in view of their links with the court of Henry II, but that would probably be a mistake. If Joseph found favour later in the court it was because of the subject-matter and the additions, but the genesis of the poem lies in the schools not in the court, especially the cathedral school at Reims. There it was that Joseph and Walter of Châtillon wrote their historical epics influenced by Lucan and Statius.[52]

Joseph of Exeter and the Court of Henry II

Although Joseph's epic was not written for the English court it needed only some minor modifications or additions to make it the sort of text that was of great interest to the Plantagenet dynasty. While it is true that the court was interested in any good story - cf. its role in the formation and diffusion of the Tristan and Iseut legend - stories of the ancient past were particularly popular both for their literary merits and for their political propaganda value. Henry II's father, Geoffrey le Bel, had been interested in his family history and was instrumental in updating the chronicles of the Counts of Angers and Vendôme, praising the dynasty's Trojan origins while deprecating the Capetians. Later additions were made, favourable to the Angevin dynasty in England,[53] possibly on Henry II's orders. These accounts were 'enlivened' and 'improved' by frequent quotations from classical authors. Furthermore, genealogical tables of the Counts of Angers were compiled to show their long, illustrious history from Trojan times, while Henry II's own education was entrusted to Peter of Saintes, author of a poem on the Trojan War. In this context must be considered Geoffrey of Monmouth's *Historia Regum Britanniae*, whatever the actual reasons that prompted Geoffrey to write it.[54] Written in 1136 and dedicated to Robert, Earl of Gloucester, uncle and guardian of Henry II from 1142 to 1147, it gives a genealogical/historical account of the kings of Britain from the first one, Brutus, great-grandson of Aeneas, to the last one, Cadwallader, who succombed to the Saxons in the 7c. The work is most famous, of course, for its account of King Arthur. In 1155 Wace translated this work into Anglo-Norman, calling it *Brut* and dedicating it to Alienor. He then undertook a sort of sequel, *Roman de Rou* or *Geste des Normands*, taking the story from Rollo, founder of the Norman dynasty, to Henry II, but was replaced by Benoit de Ste Maure who composed the *Chronique des Ducs Normands*, finishing with Henry I but managing to praise Henry I's daughter, Mathilda and her husband Geoffrey le Bel, the parents of Henry II. Thus Henry II's lineage is traced back to the founders of the Norman and Angevin dynasties, strengthening his claim to the throne of England. The Angevins descended from the Trojans; Geoffrey Gaimar's *L'Estoire des Engleis* (circa 1140) traced the royal line from Jason and the Argonauts time to William Rufus, probably establishing that the Normans were of Trojan descent too. The Trojan line from Brutus onwards had been terminated by the Saxon removal of Cadwallader, so it was only right that someone who had Trojan descent from both the Angevin and Norman sides of his family should sit on the throne of England. Henry I's attempts at the legitimation of his rule were improved upon by Henry II. Henry II appears to have wanted a fuller version of the Trojan material, and before 1170 Benoit had written the *Roman de Troie*, based on Dares, though this decision may possibly have been influenced equally by his desire to have a more historical account than that presented in the *Roman d'Eneas* which had been dedicated to Alienor about 1160. Another vernacular version of an ancient story to be written for the court was the second version of the *Roman d'Alexandre*.

Thus it is not difficult to understand how Joseph's text would fit into this context, for one can see that Latin and vernacular versions of most of the stories existed side by side at the court. For certain texts a purely historical interest probably lies behind their presence at court, but many form what was undoubtedly an unbroken chain extending from Trojan beginnings to Henry II, glorifying his lineage, providing him with a solid justification for the legitimacy of his rule and showing that he had a better literary corpus to back up his claim than the Capetians or any other royal family.

NOTES TO INTRODUCTION

1. Gompf 26, n.2; 28, n.1. The references to Joseph Iscanus in the Admont MS and to Joseph Exoniensis in the Cambridge MS cited by Manitius do not exist. They were actually formulated by modern scholars in secondary works. Consequently much that was written about Joseph's origin before 1970 is based on false information.
2. Gompf 10; G. Raynaud de Lage, *Alain de Lille*, (Montreal, 1951) 20.
3. See pp. 10-12.
4. Gompf 21.
5. Gompf 60.
6. Giraldus Cambrensis, *De Rebus a se gestis*, 2. 20.
7. A similar situation holds for Walter of Châtillon who was born at Lille, appears to have spent most of his career at Reims, yet was always known as 'de Castellione'.
8. Dom Adrian Morey, *Bartholomew of Exeter* (Cambridge, 1937), 107, thinks that the Magister Joseph who witnessed charters of Bishop Warelwast before 1160 is the author of the epic. A.L. Poole subsequently declared these charters to be dateable to the period before 1154. If the two Josephs were identical this would make the writer of the epic about 50 years old at the time of its composition, flatly contradicting the evidence of I, 15-23. He would also have been 60 when taking up his teaching post in Jodoigne and continuing his studies! Although Joseph is a rare name in the Middle Ages, a Magister Joseph, canon of Salisbury, witnessed a charter of Hilary, Bishop of Chichester, in 1147 or 1148 (cf. Mayr-Harting, *The Acta of the Bishops of Chichester*, Canterbury and York Society, vol. 56) while another is a member of Winchester Cathedral about the same time (cf. *Register of St Osmund*, Rolls Series). Bezzola III, 105 states that Joseph travelled to France in 1174 with Roger of Howden and others in the company of King Henry II, but he has misunderstood and conflated two separate statements of Stubbs (*Chronica of Roger of Hovedon*, Rolls Series, I, xv-xvi).
9. Raby 132 states this as a fact but offers no evidence for the statement.
10. Gompf 221.
11. Gompf 223. Cf. Dictionary of National Biography *sub* Joseph.
12. Gompf 225. Raby 132 incorrectly states that Guibert died in

1194. In fact, Guibert was Abbot of Florennes from 1189-94 and then Abbot of Gembloux until 1204.

13. As Gompf 20 points out, it is very difficult to understand how both Jusserand and Hutchings interpreted these lines to have been written before the death of Henry. The past tense and functions Henry had ceased to fulfill, added to the fact that these five lines are placed at the end of the encomium on the death of Hector, all point to a date after Henry's death.
14. Gompf 20-21.
15. Gompf 22. Roberts opts for 1185 because of the reference to the death of Young King Henry.
16. Gompf 9 writes of an anonymous glossator, but this is patently untrue. The glosses in A and P are sometimes contradictory. Sedgwick, 69-70, aware of only part of P, concluded 'that the nucleus proceeded from the author and was expanded by commentators with varying degrees of knowledge', basing his views on glosses that only the author could have written because the references were so abstruse and on obvious errors. A comparison of A and P show that Sedgwick's conclusions are valid. On some occasions Joseph speaks in his own voice; sometimes the glosses are verbally identical; sometimes they are verbally distinct but identical in meaning; sometimes they differ in interpretation. Furthermore, some lines in the *editio princeps* of 1541 from a now lost MS are not found in any extant MS, but are glossed.
17. For a thorough discussion of the title see Gompf 10-19.
18. Edited by J. Stohlmann, Ratingen 1968. The error is made, for example, by J. de Ghellinck, *L'Essor de la Littérature Latine au XIIe Siècle*, 1955^{2}, 437.
19. *Dares Phrygius: de excidio Troiae Historia*, ed. F. Meister, Leipzig 1873. For a survey of the influence of Dares see W. Eisenhut, 'Spätantike Troja-Erzahlungen', *Mittellateinisches Jahrbuch* 18 (1983), 1-28, and H. Homeyer, 'Beobachtungen zum Weiterleben der trojanischen Abstammungs und Gründungsagen im Mittelalter', *Respublica Litterarum* 5 (1982) 93-124.
20. I am preparing a new edition of the *Excidium Troie*.
21. Sedgwick, 60. The line-numbering that follows differs from his because he was unaware of the existence of 8 lines which the editor had suppressed or which were not in the lost MS, but I have retained his wording.
22. Sedgwick gives numerous examples of each of his observations which I have not thought fit to reproduce

here. Some are inexact because they were based on an unreliable text or on conjectures, some can be explained in different terms to his, but on the whole he is very sound.

23. Gompf 5 and 56-60.
24. Gompf 56 mentions the fact that Salutati had seen a copy in Italy. My information is that someone has discovered the first five books in a fourteenth-century MS and is still looking for the sixth. Until that is found no details will be released. One must hope that the sixth book is found fairly soon. Of course, the Italian MS may be based on one of the incomplete texts Leland saw on his travels! In any case, the fact that it is a 14th-century MS probably reduces its value for the establishing of the text. Three other MSS of a late date do exist, but they are all copies of early printed editions. Gompf 58 mentions Lüttich U.B.725 and Breslau 1652/II. To these can be added Liège 74. Short excerpts from the poem also exist in some medieval anthologies or *Florilegia*: see Gompf 51-55.
25. For a full discussion see Gompf 22-31.
26. Its value was recognised by Riddehough and Gompf.
27. Bate, 222.
28. Raby 132.
29. Gompf 221.
30. Gompf 213-19; Bate, 223-27.
31. Raby 132.
32. Gompf 61-67; Raby 133. Raby talks of two fragments but Gompf has shown that it is really one fragment that Camden cited in two parts.
33. Gompf 63 cites *Aeneis, Alexandreis*. The Antiochus in question would be the one of Maccabees 1-4.
34. Raby 133; Bezzola 3. 146-47.
35. J. Bale, *Scriptorum Illustrium Maioris Britanniae Summarium*, (Basle, 1599) iii.60, and *Index Britanniae Scriptorum*, ed. R.L. Poole (Oxford, 1902) 276-77.
36. Cf. the new ed. by M. Scaffai, *Baebii Italici Ilias Latina*, Bologna 1982.
37. For the First (and second and third) Vatican Mythographers cf. G.H. Bode, *Scriptores Rerum Mythicarum*, Celle 1834, reprinted Hildesheim 1968.
38. Around the same period a number of poems, probably rhetorical exercises, reversed the fates of the various characters in the *Iliad*. Cf. Griffin 13-14 n.2.
39. Griffin 14-15, n.1.
40. Eisenhut viii.
41. Eisenhut 134-40. A complete Greek text existed in the East

that was used by Byzantine writers.

42. Dares is cited by Isidore of Seville (d.636) and used in garbled fashion by the 7c. scribe of the Fredegar Chronicle. Cf. G. Paris, 'Historia Daretis Frigii de Origine Francorum', *Romania* 3 (1874) 129-44.
43. Cf. n.19 (Homeyer).
44. Because of Palamedes' role, the likelihood that 'Acta diurna' is a translation of 'ephemeris', and certain similarities with Greek romances.
45. Griffin 4 calls it 'an ill-assorted aggregation of meagre details'.
46. Arguments over the possible existence of a larger Dares text in the Middle Ages, used possibly by Chaucer and Benoit, have continued over the years, but the evidence is very slight.
47. E.g. Agamemnon's brother is Memnon, 'Antenor' is actually Odysseus, Pelias and Jason are at the Trojan War!
48. Atwood and Whitaker, the editors, knew of only 3 MSS but my ed. will be based on 14, of Italian, German, French and Belgian origins. Spain also had MSS but their provenance is unknown.
49. Cf. K. Schneider, *Der 'Trojanischer Krieg' im späten Mittelalter*, (Berlin 1968) 82-101 for excerpts and discussion of the Vienna MS. Atwood and Whitaker xxxi-lviii contain details of the other vernacular texts.
50. Cf. n.18 (Stohlmann 152-214) for a full discussion. I have included Benoit's vernacular *Roman de Troie* because of its important influence.
51. Ed. N.E. Griffin, *Guido de Columpnis:Historia Destructionis Troie*, (New York, 1970[2]).
52. For the presence of scholars at Reims cf. J.R. Williams, 'William of the White Hands and Men of Letters' in *Essays in Honor of C.H. Haskins* ed. C.H. Taylor (Boston, 1929) 365-87. William, the dedicatee of the *Alexandreis*, was Archbishop of Reims from 1176 to 1202. Williams does not mention Joseph.
53. Bezzola 2.327-34.
54. Cf. S. Knight, *Arthurian Literature and Society*, (London, 1983) 38-67.

SELECT BIBLIOGRAPHY

a) Joseph of Exeter

L. Gompf, *Joseph Iscanus:Werke und Briefe* (Leiden, 1970) [text]

G. Roberts, *The Iliad of Dares Phrygius* (Cape Town, 1970) [translation]

A.K. Bate, 'Joseph of Exeter, religious poet', *Medium Aevum* 41 (1971) 222-29

G. Riddehough, 'Joseph of Exeter:a forgotten poet', *JEGP* 46 (1947) 254-59

G. Riddehough, *The Text of Joseph of Exeter's Bellum Trojanum*, unpublished thesis, Harvard 1951

R.K. Root, 'Chaucer's Dares', *Modern Philology* 15 (1917) 1-22

W.B. Sedgwick, 'The Bellum Trojanum of Joseph of Exeter', *Speculum* 5 (1930) 49-76

R.R. Bezzola, *Les Origines de la littérature courtoise*, 3 vols (Paris 1958-67)

M. Manitius, *Geschichte der lateinischen Literatur des Mittelalters*, 3 vols, (Munich, 1911-31)

F.J.E. Raby, *Secular Latin Poetry*, 2 vols, (Oxford, 1957[2])

b) Contemporary or near-contemporary epics

Walter of Châtillon:Alexandreis, ed. M. Colker, (Padua, 1978)

Alberti Stadensis Troilus, ed. T. Merzdorf, (Leipzig, 1875)

Anonymi Historia Troyana Daretis Phrygii, ed. J. Stohlmann, (Ratingen, 1968)

c) Trojan War sources

Dares Phrygius:De Excidio Troiae Historia, ed. F. Meister, (Leipzig, 1873)

Dictys Cretensis:Ephemeridos Belli Troiani Libri, ed. W. Eisenhut, (Leipzig, 1973[2])

The Trojan War:the Chronicles of Dictys of Crete and Dares the Phrygian, transl. R.M. Frazer, (Bloomington, 1966)

N.E. Griffin, *Dares and Dictys*, (Baltimore, 1907)

N.E. Griffin, 'Un-Homeric elements in the medieval story of Troy', *JEGP* 7 (1908) 32-52

Excidium Troiae, ed. E.B. Attwood and V.K. Whitaker, (Cambridge, Mass. 1944)

d) Medieval poetic arts

C.S. Baldwin, *Medieval Rhetoric and Poetic*, (Gloucester, Mass. 1959[2])

E. Faral, *Les Arts poétiques du 12e et 13e siècle*, (Paris, 1962[2])

M.B. Ogle, 'Some aspects of medieval Latin style', *Speculum* 1 (1926) 170-89
W.B. Sedgwick, 'Style and vocabulary of the Latin arts of poetry', *Speculum* 3 (1928) 349-81
Grecismus Eberhardi Bethuniensis, ed. J. Wrobel, (Breslau, 1887)
T. Lawler, *The Parisiana Poetria of John of Garland* (New Haven, 1974)
E. Gallo, 'Matthew of Vendôme: Introductory Treatise on the Art of Poetry', *Proceedings of the American Philosophical Association* 118 (1974) 51-92.
The Poetria Nova of Geoffrey of Vinsauf, transl. M.F. Nims, (Toronto, 1967)

JOSEPH OF EXETER : THE TROJAN WAR

FRIGII DARETIS YLIADOS LIBER PRIMUS

PRIMA DISTINCTIO

Iliadum lacrimas concessaque Pergama fatis,
prelia bina ducum, bis adactam cladibus urbem
in cineres querimur; flemusque quod Herculis ira,
Hesiones raptus, Helene fuga fregerit arces,
impulerit Phrygios, Danaas exciverit urbes. 5
ut quid ab antiquo vatum proscripta tumultu,
veri sacra fides, longum silvescis in evum?
an, quia spreta, lates? mundoque infensa priori
nos etiam noscenda fugis? mecum, inclyta, mecum
exorere, et vultum ruga leviore resumens 10
plebeam dignare tubam: sterilisque vetustas
erubeat dum culta venis, dum libera frontem
exeris. en aures blandas, en pectus amicum
mulces, vulgarem levius passura cacchinum.
si nostris nil dulce novum, nil utile visum 15
quod teneri pariunt anni, si secula tantum
aurea Saturni memorant et nulla recentis
gratia virtutis, aude tamen ardua, pubes!
mento canescant alii, nos mente; capillo,
nos animo; facie, nos pectore. tempora certe 20
virtutem non prima negant, non ultima donant.
cumque duplex etas varios contendit in usus,
hec viget, illa iacet; hec pullulat, illa fatiscit.
Meoniumne senem, mirer, Latiumne Maronem
an vatem Phrygium Martem cui certior index 25
explicuit presens oculus, quem fabula nescit?

Book 1

My complaint is the tears of the Trojan women and Troy given up
to its fates, the two wars of the leaders, the city twice reduced
to ashes by destruction. I weep too that the anger of Hercules
destroyed its citadels, the abduction of Hesione drove on the
5 Trojans, the flight of Helen stirred up the Greek cities.
O why, exiled by the confused writings of the ancient poets,
sacred truth, have you lain hidden for so long? Are you hiding
because you were despised? Angry with former times, do you now
flee even us, when you should be recognised? With me, O famous
10 one, with me arise and adopt a countenance less marked by anger;
find my humble voice worthy of you. May the sterile past blush
with shame as you come forth adorned with culture and lift your
head in freedom. Lo, the ears you soothe are favourable to you,
the heart friendly: you will endure more easily the laughter
15 of the mob. If to our contemporaries novelty, which the present
age brings, appears to be neither pleasant nor useful, if they
recall only the Golden Age of Saturn and find no quality in recent
excellence, nevertheless dare great deeds o youth! Let others
show their age in their bearded chins, their hair and their faces
20 while I show it in my mind, my courage and my heart. Youth does
not necessarily preclude excellence nor does old age confer it;
although each age strives for different goals, youth flourishes
while old age languishes; youth multiplies while old age loses
its strength. Should I admire Homer, the old man from Maeonia,
25 or Virgil from Latium, or Dares, the Phrygian master who was
present as an eye-witness - a surer witness to describe the war
that fable does not really know?

hunc ubi combiberit avide spes ardua mentis,
quos superos in vota vocem? mens conscia veri
proscripsit longe ludentem ficta poetam,
quin te Cicropii mentita licentia pagi 30
et ledant figmenta, pater, quo presule floret
Cantia et in priscas respirat libera leges.
in numerum iam crescit honos, te tercia poscit
infula: iam meminit Wigornia, Cantia discit,
Romanus meditatur apex et naufraga Petri 35
ductorem in mediis expectat cimba procellis.
tu tamen occiduo degis contentus ovili
tertius a Thoma, Thomasque secundus, et alter
sol oriens, rebus successor, moribus heres.
felices quos non trahit ambitus! ardua nactus 40
non in se descendit honos; non ceca potestas
quid possit fortuna videt; non perfida sentit
prosperitas flevisse humilem qui ridet in altis.
parcite sacrilega superos incessere preda,
parcite! venales quisquis venatur honores 45
unde ruat tabulata struit. premit ultio noxas
tunc gravior, cum tarda venit; tunc plena timoris
cum terrore caret; blanda nil sevius ira,
cum floret miseri felix iniuria voti.
at tu dissimilis longe, cui fronte serena 50
sanguinis egregii lucrum pacemque litata
emptam anima pater ille pius, pius ille sacerdos
in curam venisse velit, cui cederet ipse
prorsus vel proprias letus sociaret habenas.

When the ambitious hope of my eager mind has absorbed this writer, what gods shall I invoke? Aware of the truth my mind has exiled to a far-off land the poet that deceives with lies, lest the lying dissoluteness of the Athenian Areopagus and its fictions should offend you, father, - you the prelate under whom Canterbury flourishes and free, breathes again in its former rights. Your honour is reaching its fulfillment. A third ecclesiastical dignity calls you: Worcester now remembers you, Canterbury is getting to know you, the Roman diadem has you in mind. The shipwrecked boat of Peter waits for its captain in the middle of the storm, yet you live content with your western flock, the third after Thomas but a second Thomas, another rising sun, his temporal successor and moral heir. Happy are those whom ambition does not lead on! Having scaled the heights honour does not descend into itself; blind power does not see what fortune can do; perfidious prosperity does not feel if the man who laughs at the top wept when he was at the bottom. Cease to attack the saints with sacrilegious gains! Cease! Whoever hunts for venal honours is building platforms for his downfall. Vengeance dogs the guilty, more dire when coming late; then it is to be feared utterly when it lacks fear. There is nothing crueller than its smiling anger when injustice is successful in pursuit of an evil wish and flourishes. But you are far different, you to whose care with serene face that pious father, that pious priest would have wished to come what he earned with his noble blood, the peace bought by the offering of his soul. To you he would have been glad to hand over his control directly or to share it with you.

hactenus hec, tuque, oro, tuo da, maxime, vati 55
ire iter inceptum Trioamque aperire iacentem!
te sacre assument acies divinaque bella
tunc dignum maiore tuba, tunc pectore toto
nitar et immensum mecum spargere per orbem.

Narratio

Luserat omnifice quondam sollertia cure 60
ignotas molita rates, aurique cupido
audendi transgressa modum trans equora misit,
qui raperent thalamos, spoliarent templa metallis.
siccine mortalis finem metitur hiatus?
egeste sic Ditis opes, quas ambitus audax, 65
quas predo pallens Stygiis extorquet ab antris,
sufficiunt? cui iam satis est, quod regna, quod urbes
ipsaque quod pateant rapiendis Tartara gazis?
itur in ignotos fluctus, ultroque procellis
insultare iuvat et soli vivere fato. 70

Profectio Argonautarum ad Colchon insulam

Esonides primus undas assumsit in usus
Phryxeam rapturus ovem, cui laudis alumnus
Alcides socias indulsit in ardua vires,
his Peleus Telamonque duces, his cetera pubes
Emathie. casus pelagi coniurat in omnes 75
pars mirata ratem, pars fame prona petende,
pars mundum visura novum gentesque remotas.
ergo sequi docilis quas nondum noverat undas

Enough of that; I pray you, O mighty one, allow your bard to continue the journey he has begun and to reveal the destruction of Troy. The holy armies and religious wars will then take you, worthy of a greater song; then with all my strength will I strive and your fame will spread worldwide with me.

Narrative

Long ago the ingenuity of all-producing care had been at play building boats that were previously unknown to man, and greed for gold, going beyond the bounds of audacity, sent men across the seas to steal a bride and despoil temples of their gold. Is it thus that human greed measures its end? Did not the riches of Pluto, mined from the earth and hewn out of the Stygian caves by the bold ambition of the pallid plundering miner, suffice? For whom now then is it enough that kingdoms, cities and even Hell itself allow their riches to be stolen? Men ventured into unknown waters and moreover rejoiced in facing storms and living by fate alone.

The Departure of the Argonauts for the Isle of Colchis

Jason, son of Aeson, first used the sea for his own ends in going to steal the Golden Fleece. With him went Hercules, grandson of Alceus but foster-son of fame, who accepted to lend his strength for the difficulties ahead, and with these the dukes Peleus and Telamon together with the rest of the youth of Thessaly. A common oath, whatever the dangers of the sea, was sworn by some who admired the boat, others keen on earning fame and others who wanted to see a new world and distant peoples. So, ready to follow the seas it had never known,

Tetios in gremium migrat prerepta Diane
pinus et e ramis remos habet, inque profundum 80
ornatu contenta rudi - plus robore, cultu
fisa minus - paucis exul peregrinat in armis.
nondum seva deos ponto obiectare natantes
relligio, non fluxa sinu tumuere superbo
carbasa. delicias dat fastiditior usus 85
exornatque suum novitas operosa periclum.
prima inopem pinus cultum quo stabat in Hemo
detulit in Syrtes. auctor ratis Argus, et Argo
navis erat, sed uterque rudis. nil illa superbe,
non auro superos lesit, non rupibus aurum. 90

Iter Iasonis ad rapiendum aureum vellus

Stat dubius novus hospes aque, reditumque fugamque
ludentis pelagi miratur, et equora visu
metitur, patrieque pium consultat amorem
virtuti nutu facili cessurus et undis.
sed rapit aura ratem. quonam, quo naufraga tendis? 95
quo populos in fata trahis? tene angue vel armis
patrandum fastidit opus? scio: tedia tollis,
delicias leti queris. nunc utere saxo,
terra potens, atque iniecte Symplegadis ictu
nulla prius consumta refer! ferat ipsa cruentum 100
quod peperit fatum, primaque superbiat ira!
fata obstant, hominum predatrix Atropos arcet.
plus superi quam vota queunt; trabs Thessala divos
presentes, quos fecit, habet. Contemtus in antris

the pine-tree boat, felled in the forest of Diana, proceeded into
30 the lap of Thetis and its oars were branches. Content with rough
decoration and little equipment she went into exile on the main,
trusting more in her strength, less in her sophistication. As yet
cruel religion had not imposed gods bobbing on the sea nor did
billowing linen sails yet swell into the shape of noble breasts.
35 Familiarity bringing tedium in turn produces refinements and
inventive novelty gilds its danger. The first boat brought to the
Syrtes the unwrought elegance it had as a pine tree on Mount Haemus.
The builder of the boat was Argus, the boat itself the Argo;
both were unpolished. The Argo was not arrogant, she did not harm
90 the gods with gold nor the gold with rocks.

Journey of Jason to steal the Golden Fleece

The new guest of the sea stands there hesitating, wondering at the
ebb and flow of the playful sea. He gauges the expanse of the sea
with his eye, thinks of his natural love for his country, ready to
95 abandon easily both fame and sea. But the wind catches the boat.
Where, oh where are you making for, wrecker? Where are you dragging
peoples to their doom? Does murder to be carried out by poison
or weapons bore you? I know you are relieving your boredom,
you are seeking refinements in death. Now use a stone, o powerful
earth, and with a blow from the clashing Symplegades forget any
100 previously unsuccessful means of death. Let the Argo suffer
the bloody fate she made possible and glory in the first anger!
But the fates do not agree, Atropos, the huntress of men, forbids.
The gods can achieve more than my prayers; the Thessalian boat
has the gods she created around her. In his cave

Ypotades, in aquis Triton, in carcere Corus 105
hac rate prerepta summos senuisset in annos.
quippe deum genitore metu mens ceca creavit
Ditem umbris, celo superos et numina ponto.
vix pelagi sensere minas, iamque 'Eole' clamant,
'Eole tuque dato mulces qui cerula sceptro, 110
undarum Neptune potens, date numen ituris!
si reduces, meritis nomen sacrabitur aris.'
mox certant in vota dei gaudentque vocati;
hic faciles proclinat aquas, hic evocat antro
qui vela impregnet Zephirum, qui purget abacta 115
nube diem. cursu tandem producta sereno
labitur in portus Phrygios ratis, improba pubes
emicat, et vetita certant tellure potiri.

Fama nocens subitum Segea in regna tumultum
spargit, et insidias populo regique minatur, 120
Dardana si coeant peregrine ad litora classes.
plebs excita furit; nec abest qui Laomedontem
intentet Danais, ultro ni litore cedant.
o superis invisa manus! sic pignora celi
crescentesque deos in Syrtes cogis? an unam 125
extimeas gens tanta ratem? sed, ceca, quid horres?
huc hospes, non hostis, adest, cui monstra potenti
debentur frangenda manu. reverere Tonantem
vel saltem cognosce hominem! si pendimus equum,
si rerum iustis metimur partibus usum, 130
omne homini commune solum. sed iura perosus
publica sacrilegis naturam barbarus ausis

05 Aeolus, son of Hippotes, in the sea Triton, in his prison
Corus, each would have grown old, despised for eternity if
this boat had been forcibly removed earlier. Indeed, with
fear as the creator of the gods, man's blind mind put Pluto
in the underworld, gods in the sky and powers in the sea.
Scarcely had they sensed the dangers of the sea when they
10 shouted 'Aeolus, Aeolus, and you, Neptune, lord of the waves,
who have been given the power to calm the seas, give your
approval to us as we set out! If we return, your name will be
revered on worthy altars.' Immediately the gods compete to
fulfill their prayers, happy to be called upon; Neptune smoothes
15 down the waves to make them easy, Aeolus calls Zephyrus out of
the cave to make the sail big and to clear the sky by blowing
away the clouds. At last, carried along in its uneventful course
the boat slips into the Phrygian harbours; the headstrong youths rush
out of the boat and struggle to get a foothold on the forbidden land.

Evil rumour suddenly spreads tumult in the Trojan kingdom,
20 threatening the people and their king with danger if foreign fleets
should come to Trojan shores. The people get excited and angry; and
someone is ready to turn Laomedon against the Greeks if they do not
agree to leave the beach. O people hated by the gods! Is it thus
that you drive on to the dangers of the sea these men not only beloved
by the gods but also destined to become gods themselves? Are you,
25 a great nation, to be frightened by one boat? But, blind people, what do
you fear? This is a guest not an enemy. His powerful hands will
destroy monsters. Fear Jupiter the Thunderer or at least show
Hercules some humanity! If we are fair, if we are impartial in
30 sharing out the world for use, every land is common to all mankind.
But the barbarian, hating international laws with his sacrilegious daring

contrahit, et proprios Phrygiam phariseat in usus.
o Asie pollentis opes! o Pergama nulli
tranquillo cessura deo! nil dura sororum 135
licia, nil superi peccant; gens incola fatum
ipsa facit, celo Phrygius parcente meretur
exilium, gladios, incendia. pellitur Argo
armatumque Iovem mediis exorat in undis.
at Danai flagrant, animis poscentibus arma, 140
quo rapit ira sequi gladioque ultore pudendam
excusare fugam. contra prudentia, turbe
rara comes, raro Phrygiam cum milite pendit.
excipit ancipites docti tuba Nestoris aures,
suspensosque regit irataque pectora mulcet: 145

Sermo Nestoris

'O qui magnanimo domuistis remige fluctus,
qui freta, qui ventos primi libastis et astra
iratum didicistis iter non nota secuti,
discite dura pati! sola est que conterit hostem
virtutesque regit patientia; sola triumphis 150
militat innocuis et honeste consulit ire.
est tempus quando, locus est ubi. ledimur omnes,
ledimur immeriti patimurque indigna priores
ut causa meliore frui superisque secundis
marte dato liceat. non hec iniuria nobis 155
sed Danais facta est. veniet qui probra suorum
ense pio redimat.' sic fatur, et accipit omnes
delinita Thetis gremiumque exponit ituris.

reduces nature's gifts by setting apart Phrygia for Phrygians only.
O riches of powerful Asia! O Pergamum, you who will yield to no
35 god in time of peace! It is not the fault of the strong threads
of the Fates nor of the gods above. The inhabitants are making
their own destiny; the Trojan is now earning exile, slaughter and
conflagrations whereas previously the gods were indulgent.
The Argo is driven off and from out in the sea the Greeks pray
40 to Jupiter the Avenger. But as their hearts yearn for weapons the
Greeks burn to follow where their anger leads them and to make
amends for their shameful flight by the sword's revenge. Against
this, however, prudence, rarely found in a large mob, contrasted
the whole of Phrygia with the few Greek soldiers. The words of
45 wise Nestor came to their ears as they hesitated, guided their
uncertainty and calmed their angry hearts.

Nestor's Speech

'O you who have tamed the waves with your heroic rowing, who first
made trial of the sea and the winds, following unknown stars to
discover the dangers of this journey, now learn to put up with
50 hardships! Patience is the only means of governing one's strengths
and defeating the enemy; it alone fights for bloodless triumphs and
has respect for righteous anger. There is a right time, a right
place. We have all been slighted - unfairly so - and we are first
suffering indignities so that our cause will be better and the gods
55 favourable once war has started. This insult has been inflicted not
on us alone but on the Greeks as a whole. There will come a man who
will avenge with his pious sword the disgraceful repulse of his
fellow-countrymen.' Thus he spoke and the sea now deflowered took
on all comers, exposing her lap to any traveller.

Iam fluctus emensa vagos in Phasidis undas
declinat Pegasea ratis pelagoque relicto, 160
pauperiore sinu sed liberiore potita
multa prius metuenda tulit dum litore in alto
discordes agerent undarum prelia motus.
improbus audaci suspendit gurgite pontum
Phasis et obnitens castigat in arva ruentem 165
cessuram miseratus humum. furit ille feroxque
potandas incestat aquas bilemque refundit
in vada blanda suam dedignaturque teneri.
ipsa etiam clausisque Nothis celoque sereno
continuas hiemes portus angustia volvit, 170
nec spatio laxum languet mare; crescit arena
consumptura rates tellusque occulta vadosas
in cumulum suspendit aquas mentita profundum.
fluctuat ambiguus Tiphys, prope litora spectat,
suspectam formidat humum discitque timere 175
quo tutum sperabat iter. timor elicit artem.
consultura vadum medias minor alnus in undas
pellitur et conto metitur iudice pontum.
litoris insidie postquam patuere, coacto
inter utrumque solum decurrens limite puppis 180
arva petita premit fractasque offendit arenas.

Quid memorem Esonide duras incumbere leges
Oethe imperio, quid semina iacta, quid hostes
terrigenas Martisque boves sevique draconis
excubias? ignis virtuti cedit et ensis 185
eripiturque emptum summo discrimine vellus.

And now, having journeyed over the moving waves, the swift boat
160 turned into the waters of the River Phasis. With the sea behind her
she came into a creek that was shallower but less dangerous, although
first she had to contend with many frights as conflicting currents
battled against each other on the steeply-shelving beach. The bold
165 River Phasis with its brave waters held back the sea, struggling to
check it as it rushed towards the fields, for the river took pity
on the vulnerable land. The sea raged and wildly muddied the clear
water, pouring its filth into the fresh river water in its anger at
being countered. Even in the absence of winds when the sky is clear
170 the narrowness of the harbour created continual eddies as the broad
sea found no rest in the confined space: the sandbanks increase as
though to overwhelm boats, and the unseen bottom heaps up the
shallows, giving a false appearance of depth. Tiphys hesitates, in
175 two minds what to do: he looks at the shore near at hand, is afraid of
suspected ground and even learns to be afraid where he hoped the
passage was safe. Fear brings out his skill. A smaller craft is rowed
out into the middle of the waves to test the shoals and the depth of
the water is measured with a measuring rod. When the dangers of the
180 shore were known, the boat slips along a narrow channel between two
banks, beaches up on the land she sought, scattering the sand as she
drives in.

Why should I recount the harsh terms imposed on Jason, son of Aeson,
by Aeetes' orders, or the seeds that were sown, or the earthborn
185 adversaries, or the bulls of Mars, or the watchfulness of the cruel
dragon? Fire yielded to courage, as did the sword, while the fleece
that was earned by such signal combat was removed.

Neptunum sensisse putes; fugientibus equor
altius intumuit fractique in litora fluctus
intonuere simul: 'Procul, o procul ite profani!
non licet in sanctum cum preda tendere pontum.' 190
has Nothus haut passus causas instare timoris
preripuit voces nec iter concessit in aures.

Reditus Iasonis cum aureo vellere

Navigat auricomo spoliatis vellere Colchis
predo potens. culpemne ratem que prima per undas
ad facinus molita vias atque Atropon auxit, 195
an causa potiore probem? sine remigis usu
non nosset Memphis Romam, non Indus Hiberum,
non Schita Cicropidem, non nostra Britannia Gallum.
primus ab excubiis montes proreta Pelasgos
anticipat salvere iubens, at cetera pubes 200
remorum assurgit studio victrixque carina
Thessalicis reddit, quos in freta duxerat, arvis.
quis varios memoret plausus, quis gaudia vulgi?
si parcus meminisse velim, vel nolle fateri
vel seriem non nosse putent; si prodigus, auris 205
fastidita neget faciles ad singula nutus.
Pelea miratur reducem Larissa Pilonque
Nestor habet, Thelamone suo Salamina superbit,
Leda Terauneis et fratribus Orithia
Ysmariis laudatque suum Calidonia mater 210
Oenidem, nondum tantum soror, Orphea Traces,
Archades Admetum, Thalaumque et Thesea et Idam

You would think Neptune was aware of the deed. The water piled up higher in front of the fugitives while the waves breaking on the shore
190 thundered in unison: 'Keep away, keep well away, you evil men! It is not permitted to sail on the divine sea with plunder.' The wind did not allow these frightening words to affect the Argonauts but instead snatched them away and did not let them reach their ears.

Return of Jason with the Golden Fleece

The powerful pirate sails away with the Golden Fleece that had been
195 stolen from the Colchians. Should I condemn the boat that first made its way through the waves to crime and increased deaths, or should I commend it for a greater reason? If it were not for the use of oars Memphis would not have known Rome, nor India Spain, nor Scythia Athens, nor our Britain France. The look-out on the prow is first
200 to make out the mountains of Greece and he gives the signal to cheer, but the rest of the young heroes merely row harder and the victorious boat returns to the fields of Thessaly those it had carried out on to the seas. Who could recount all the kinds of cheering or the people's joy? If I were to say little on the subject readers might think I was
205 unwilling to describe it, or else that I did not know the details. If, however, I were wordy, the bored listener would refuse to approve of everything. Larissa is surprised at the return of Peleus; Nestor regains Pylos; Salamis revels in its Telamon, Leda in her Spartan sons,
210 Orithyia in her Ismarian brothers, while the Calydonian mother, not yet merely a sister, praises Meleager, her son by Oeneus. The Thracians applaud Orpheus, the Arcadians Admetus. Thalaus, Theseus and Idas

Antheumque urbes varie, sua menia quemque.
at Peloponensum cum preda divite Iason
occupat. insigni lascivit regia cultu 215
victorique suo gratas plebs obvia voces
elicit et vero dispensant gaudia vultu.
solus inexplicita Pelias sub fronte serena
invidia egrescit, sese causatur, in omnes
vota deos consumpta gemit Martemque lacessit, 220
qui gratis domitos tulerit defervere tauros.
eluctata diu rapidis impulsibus ira
in verbum singultat atrox questusque superbos:

Questus Pelie de reditu Iasonis

'O superi, quo thura meant? o fata, quis error
imperat? o hominum casus, paucosne reservat 225
ut multos fortuna premat? iam sentio, traxi
invito mea regna deo. cape, maxime, tandem
quorum fastidit usus regnare negantem,
que longo emisti voto, tumeasque relictis,
non raptis. tenui certe non sponte deorum 230
hisque velim regnis emptum vicisse Tonantem.
me mage - si qua fides - votorum offensa lacessit
quam sceptri iactura mei. voluine sub Arcton
proscripsisse virum? regnat. fregisse? superbit.
extinxisse? viget. titulos minuisse? triumphat. 235
ergo deos dita ingratos, da thura Tonanti:
cum dederis, sperata neget, donisque retentis
rideat elusum. melius fortuna pianda est,

and Anthaeus are welcomed by various cities - each their own. But
Jason with his rich plunder enters Peloponensus. The palace is
15 festive and splendidly decorated, the people come to greet their
hero with gratitude, their faces showing genuine joy. Only Pelias
is sick with jealousy, though he hides this behind a happy facade.
20 He blames himself, bemoans the fact that he had wasted his prayers
on all the gods, and rails against Mars who had allowed his bulls
to be tamed into inaction although he had been offered nothing.
After seething for some time his anger breaks out savagely in rapid
sobbing bursts into arrogant words of complaint:

<u>Complaints of Pelias about Jason's return</u>

'O gods above, where does incense go? O fates, what mistake rules?
25 O chance, does fortune save a few men in order to destroy many? Now
I realise that I have ruled my kingdom longer than Jupiter wished.
Mighty Jupiter, take those things whose enjoyment finally palls
on one who refuses to reign, those things that you have prayed for
for so long. Now puff yourself up with pride over what has been
30 handed over to you, not acquired by your own efforts. I have been
king not by the will of the gods and I should have liked to defeat
Jupiter by bribing him with this kingdom. The spurning of my prayers
angers me more - if you can believe that - than the loss of my rule.
Did I want to banish the man to the far north? He is king.
35 To break him? He is glorious. To destroy him? He is flourishing.
To diminish his fame? He is triumphant. So, enrich the ungrateful
gods, send incense up to Jupiter: when you have done so, then may he
dash your hopes, keep your gifts and mock you when he has made a
fool of you. It is better to propitiate Fortune

que pacem, que fulmen habet, que prima tyrannis
imperium partita tribus concessit, abegit, 240
mutato lusit celo, rursusque iubebit
quos fecit reges, mecum migrare sub umbras,
et Iove proscripto Saturni leniet iras.'
sic fatur, diroque animam depascitur estu.
has tamen, has cordis rugas, hec prelia mentis 245
frontis oliva domat, faciesque dolosa sophistam
mendicat vultum et blandos peregrinat in usus.

Gaudia prima ducum sollempni mensa tumultu
excipit. at celi predo terreque marisque,
ambitus, acceptas venatur regibus escas: 250
Iuno liram volucrum languescere sentit; alumnos
equoris emungi Thetis dolet: aspera Phebe
indignata sui numerum rarescere civis
excubat ultoremque humeris accommodat arcum,
venantes venata viros predamque petentes 255
in predam petit et lucos vigilantius ambit.
ergo thoros conviva premit donumque dearum
interpres blandus hilarat deus humida siccis
mire concilians. comptos discreta clientes
cura agit; hi Cererem cumulant, hi fercula mutant, 260
illi hilares iterant calices. at rege superbo
emeritum libante merum mensalibus herent
submissique haustum Bacchi regalis adorant.

Has mense genialis opes, hec ocia cure
dapsilis, hoc grati certamen dulce laboris 265
incolumi virtus delibat sobria gustu.

who holds peace and the thunderbolt in her hands, who first shared
40 out power between the three tyrants, drove out Saturn, played under
a changed heaven, and once again will command the kings she created
to descend with me into the underworld. She will banish Jupiter and
calm the anger of Saturn.' Thus he spoke and he nourishes his mind
45 with the fire of his wrath. However, this shrivelled heart, this
turbulent mind, are masked by his calm appearance; his deceitful face
borrowed a false look, a gentle expression that was foreign to him.

A banquet with its festive revelry follows the leaders' first joy. But
50 greed, that robber of sky, earth and sea, hunts fare fit for kings.
Juno feels the birdsong weaken in volume; Thetis is sad that the sea's
inhabitants are diminishing; Phoebe, angry that her subjects are
getting fewer, keeps watch, fits the avenging bow to her shoulder.
55 Hunting the hunters she seeks as prey those who are seeking prey,
stalking her woods with more care than usual. So the guests sit down,
and Bacchus, the sweet go-between, happily mixed with the goddesses'
gifts of food, thus producing a wonderful marriage of liquid and solid.
60 Different tasks occupy the well-dressed servants; some pile up the
bread, some serve new dishes, while others refill the joyous goblets.
But as the arrogant king drinks some vintage wine they stand around
with their napkins and dutifully applaud the royal drinking. This
65 richness of magnificent food, these generous offerings of affection
and leisure, this tasty match of love and effort are savoured by the
sober and virtuous who keep their tastebuds intact.

non ignava gravi peperere oblivia menti
delicie, non in sompnos elanguit ira
Amphitrioniade. Troiam bis terque resumens
se vultu reserat animumque his asperat egrum: 270

Conquestio Herculis

'Ergo Iovem meritus cunali Marte parentem
celestes docui mecum vagire dracones
prevenique minas? pudet, heu, vir, victor, adultus
barbaricis cessi, non viso milite, iussus.
ergo minis frangendus eram? pro fata pudenda! 275
pro crimen superum! fato Iunonior omni
nescio quis fame meritum scidit. arma tenebam,
nec deerant hostes. i nunc, et prisca revolvens
privignum mirare tuum, Iovis inclita coniunx!
vicisti, fateor, fugi; victoria summa 280
Alciden fugisse fuit. rursusne severum
dignere artificem nostris Euristea penis?
si Lernam edomui, si Cerberus ore trifauci
in scopulos, Dodona, tuos aconita refudit,
si gravis Antheus gratam suspensus arenam 285
dedidicit mirante Rea, si cetera mundi
monstra triumphali potui consumere dextra,
in Frigios - dicamne viros? - humanaque bella
depotuisse pudet. sed cur clare acta revolvo?
degeneri gravius accedit gloria facto. 290
quin potius seris gladius quid conferat ausis,
monstrorum domitor, reminiscere! Pergama penas

But the revelries do not produce base forgetfulness in an anxious mind: the anger of Hercules, son of Amphitryon, does not die away into sleep. Two or three times he thinks again of Troy, his feelings for

270 all to see on his face as he reproached his afflicted heart with these thoughts:

The Complaint of Hercules

'So, when I fought that battle in the cradle did I not deserve to be able to call Jupiter my father? Did I not teach the snakes sent from heaven to cry like me? Did I not forestall a threat on my life? It is shameful, alas, that a man, a mature hero, has been ordered to yield to

275 barbarians without seeking any fighting. So should I be browbeaten by mere threats? O shameful fates! O, the crime of the gods! Someone crueller than all the fates has destroyed my well-earned reputation. I had weapons and the enemy was at hand. Go on, famous wife of Jupiter, think of your stepson's former deeds and be dumbstruck! You won, I

280 admit it. I fled. Hercules' flight was your greatest victory. Will you again enlist Eurystheus, the cruel instigator of my labours? If I tamed Lerna, if Cereberus vomited up from his three throats the

285 poison on to your rocks, Dodona, if heavy Antaeus, held aloft, forgot the strength-giving earth to the amazement of Rea, if I was able to overcome with my triumphant right hand the other monsters of the world, then it is a disgrace for me to have renounced mere human war against Trojan - what shall I call them? - men. But why do I recall my

290 famous deeds? Glory does not really suit an ignoble deed. You slayer of monsters, why not remember rather what the sword may bring with acts of daring, even if they are late? Let Pergamum pay the penalty

pendant et meritis periuros perde ruinis,
sic Phebo liquidoque Iovi ducture triumphum,
sic tibi, sic Danais! docilesque instare Pelasgos 295
non fugisse sciant, qui, cum potuere minari,
et potuere pati!" tacitis sic questibus iram
exacuens summos animum procudit in ausus.
haut secus exilium grate dequestus arene
armenti princeps lunatum robur in ornos 300
asperat obiectas et se premensus in hostem
ocia dura gerit et prelia pulcra figurat
fronte furens pulsasque pudet non frangere silvas.
inde thoro meliore redit veteremque repulsam
excusans victor regnat lauroque superbit. 305

Apparatus Herculis ad bellum

Vix primos belli motus libraverat heros
et iam fama loquax rapiens ex aure potentum
quod serat in vulgus, pavidas quod spargat in urbes,
prelia mota canit. illamne nocentis Averni
progeniem celine rear, que murmura rerum 310
occulta extenebrat redditque latentia luci?
immo quis e supera contendat pace creatam
turbatricem hominum que sancta silentia regum
in mundi perfert aures et plebis in ora
dissipat archanum cure furata silentis? 315
haut mora, non lituis iussi, non ere vocati,
conspirant ad bella viri; sed et arma tumultu
plebs rapit, et vibrans quos non bene noverat enses,

while you slaughter the perjurers with the destruction they deserve, thus gaining a triumph for Apollo, for the sea-god as well as for you and the Greeks! And may they learn that the Greeks did not flee but are ready to attack. Those who were able to threaten once were also able to suffer.' With these silent complaints thus fuelling his anger he strengthened his resolve for the utmost daring. In like fashion does the leader of the herd, bemoaning his exile from his beloved territory, fiercely stimulate the strength of his horns on the ash-trees in his way, and practising against an eventual enemy he finds the lack of activity hard to put up with. Imagining splendid contests, the bull rages with his horns and does not disdain to break the trees he attacks. He returns from exile with greater strength, redeems his former defeat and boasts of his success as a victorious ruler.

Hercules' Preparations for War

Scarcely had Hercules given some thought to the initial preparation for war when babbling Rumour, snatching from the councils of the powerful what she can divulge to the public and spread around in frightened cities, tells that war has begun. Shall I consider her to be the offspring of evil hell or or heaven, she who brings out of the shadows clandestine discussions and exposes secrets to the light of day? But who would argue that this upsetter of men was created in heavenly peace? She, I mean, who brings to the ears of the world and spreads in the mouths of the people the revered secrets of kings, robbing the unknown hiding-place of the unspoken thought! Immediately, without any orders from trumpet or command from bugle, men agree on war; but the mob takes up arms in chaotic fashion, wielding swords it does not really know how to use.

ingenue irasci discit multumque minatur,
sed factura parum. terit hic in frena iugales 320
non longum mansurus eques; rapta ille superbit
casside, at impatiens captos decrescere visus.
hi suras riguisse stupent; hi pondere victi
in clipeos nutant. pars barbara regna lacessit
litigiis audax et citra prelia fortis, 325
obiecto secura freto. gemit anxia matrum
turba, nec infaustis solacia mesta querelis
ire negant lacrime, lacrimis certatur et omnem
excessisse putat flendi parcissima luctum.
hec inter medios enses timet; illa Caribdim 330
incurrit: pietas numquam secura quiescit.
mens o prona virum! non hec suspiria virtus
infracta admittit, non dant complexibus artus,
oscula non iterant, ne vel sic bella morentur,
vix memores dixisse: 'vale'. mulcetur alumpnus 335
fatorum Alcides et spe meliore superbis
assidet inceptis. fremitu navalia fervent
Egeosque sinus ter quino remige frangit
lecta cohors totidemque movet per cerula pinus.
at Nothus incumbens humeris puppique sequaci 340
ducit inoffensam Simoontis in hostia classem.

Bellum Herculis et Troianorum

Puppibus emigrat primus, Thelamone secundo,
Larisse pollentis honos, cui cerula nupsit
Nereis, amplexus non aspernata minores

It learns noble anger, threatening much but destined to achieve
20 precious little. One budding knight forces a bridle on a horse, but
he will not stay mounted long. Another struts around in a stolen helmet
but cannot stand the restricted vision. Others are amazed at the
stiffness of their legs with greaves on. Others yet fall forward on
to their shields because the weight is too much for them. Yet more
25 utter threats at the kingdom of the barbarians, brave in their insults
and strong before the fight, safe as they are with the sea in between.
The worried crowd of mothers groan, and their tears, that sad
consolation for unlucky laments, do not refuse to flow, so much so,
30 in fact, that a weeping contest ensues and even the driest-eyed thinks
she has outdone all the others in her grief. One mother fears for her
son in combat, another sees Charybdis as an obstacle: never does a
mother's love remain carefree and untroubled. O headstrong mind of man!
Unbroken manliness does not accept these sighs nor welcome embraces; it
35 does not give a second kiss in case war should be held up by it. These
men hardly remember to say farewell. Hercules, grandson of Alceus and
foster-child of the fates, is happy at this and with enhanced hope sets
about his proud endeavour. The shipyards bustle with excitement as the
chosen band of rowers breaks the surface of the Aegean sea with their
fifteen oars, and the same number of boats sails through the waters.
40 But the south wind blows on their shoulders from behind the stern and
brings the fleet unimpeded into the harbour of the Simois.

Hercules' War against the Trojans

First out of the ships, closely followed by Telamon, is Peleus, the pride
of powerful Larissa, whom the sea-goddess, Thetis the Nereid, married,
not despising an inferior marriage

mortalemque thorum, quo principe gloria spirat 345
Mirmidonum, quem tota suis obnoxia fatis
Dorica castra canunt. Danais hic debet Achillem,
Aiacem Thelamon, equale in Pergama fulmen.
dividit ergo acies equi libraminis instar
Alcides: pars in Frigios armata Penates 350
iam dictos sortita duces, pars cura relicte
classis disponit cum Nestore, parsque secuta
Amphitrioniadem sociis partitur utrisque
excubias hinc inde suas. sic agmine trino
consulitur bello. patriumque armaverat orbem 355
principis edictum Frigii, ruit omnis in arma
barbaries; flammisque rates consumere fisus
et Danaos sparsurus aquis ad litora martem
dux migrare iubet, paretur et ocius omnes
fluctibus insiliunt. solite nil tale timere 360
Nereides visa arma stupent horrentque tumultum.
hi telis instant, alii face; pectora telum,
fax puppes iniecta petit; cunabula Mavors
Cypridis infestat armis et Lennius igne.
tunc primum bellis rubuit mare: sanguinis illas 365
murex hausit opes, quas nondum oblitus in annos
presentes meminit regumque expendit in usum.
Scilleos nova preda canes ad funera mesti
gurgitis invitat, coeunt latrantibus undis
monstra sinus Siculi, dehinc hausto nectare diro 370
in freta sparguntur similem venantia potum.
at fremitu accepto Nereus excussus ab antris

345 nor a mortal husband. Under his kingship the glory of the Mirmidons
flourishes. It is he that the whole Greek army praises, although it
is prejudicial to his fates. Peleus owes Achilles to the Greeks, Telamon
owes Ajax, to be twin thunderbolts against Troy. Hercules divides up
350 his battle forces in equal parts: one part is detailed to join an armed
attack against the city of Troy under the leadership of the
aforementioned generals, Peleus and Telamon; the second is marshalled
under Nestor to protect the anchored fleet; the third follows Hercules,
355 dividing the watches between two groups. Thus a threefold strategy
of war is evolved. An edict of the Phrygian king had put all his
territory under arms, so all the barbarians rush to take up their weapons.
Counting on burning the ships and scattering the Greeks in the sea
360 Laomedon forms his battle line up on the beach. The order is obeyed
quickly by all the Trojans who leap into the waves. The Nereids are
amazed and horrified on seeing the weapons and the tumult as they are
not accustomed to fearing anything like it. Some men attack with spears,
others with firebrands. Spears are thrown at bodies, firebrands at
ships. Mars attacks the sea, the birthplace of Venus, with arms
365 while Vulcan uses fire. Then for the first time the sea turned red
through warfare: the purple-fish absorbed those huge quantities of
blood that it has not yet forgotten, remembering it up to the present
day and providing it for the benefit of kings. This new prey
attracts the dogs of Scylla to the corpses of the sorrowing sea.
370 These monsters of the Gulf of Sicily come together in the barking
waves, drink the grim nectar and then disperse all over the sea
hunting for a similar drink. When he hears the uproar Nereus is
roused from his cavern.

mutatis horrescit aquis, fontique relapsus
nascentem explorat urnam, visoque meatu
quem genitrix Natura dedit, securior exit. 375
immo agite, inmisso bellum consumite ponto,
dii si qui undarum, rapteque Athlante repulso
evolvantur aque! fatis iniuria prima
excusanda fuit, an et hos impune furores
ferre iuvat? misero complutus sanguine pontus 380
spumat et incensum fumat mare. Scilla Caribdim
excitat et nostris pinguescunt monstra ruinis.
si neutros superesse ratum, si iudice causa
elicitis penas, Frigios periuria mergent,
exemplum sceleris Danaos. que iam mora, segnes? 385
pronius in facinus tardis ultoribus itur.

Ardua iam trepidis murorum septa catervis
Iliace cinxere manus. stat Dardana pubes
pro iugulis armata suis; nec enim invida regni
ambitio ludit pugnas, sed et ira mineque 390
et non extorti per vulnera cruda furores
bella cient hinc inde odiis flammata superbis.
primus in adversos librata cuspide muros
torquet equum Peleus fractaque accenditur hasta.
'hac' ait 'hospitiis aditus et in hospita tecta 395
pulsanti reseranda manu. nos urbe fruamur,
portu alii.' dixit, cunctique instare Pelasgi,
ceu belli tunc causa recens nec tempore longo
ira minor. minus accendant in prelia mentes

Horrified at the changed nature of the waters he slips back to
investigate the wellsprings of the ocean, and having verified the
375 source that Mother Nature gave, he returns more confidently. Come on,
you gods of the sea, if you exist, destroy the combatants with a flood
of your waters. Remove Atlas and let the divided waters rush together!
The first insult had to be excused by the fates, but are they now
380 accepting this madness without taking any action? Permeated by pitiful
human blood the sea foams and the heated ocean steams. Scylla arouses
Charybdis and the monsters grow fat on our disasters. If the judgement
is that neither nation should survive, if you demand punishment to fit
the crime, then their perjuries will drown the Trojans and their model
385 for criminality the Greeks. What is the delay, you laggards? Crime is
bolder when vengeance is slow.

The Trojan people were already huddled around the steep fortifications
of their walls in trembling groups. The Trojan young men stand armed to
390 defend their throats: for this is not envious ambition for a kingdom
practising warfare, but anger and threats and rage not produced by cruel
wounds incite the fighting inflamed by the hate and arrogance of both
sides. Peleus is the first to turn his horse toward the enemy walls,
395 throwing his spear and then bursting into anger when the spear breaks.
'This is the way' he shouts, 'to hospitality and the guestrooms that
will be unlocked when we knock on the door. Let us enjoy the city
while the others enjoy the harbour.' When he finished speaking all
the Greeks attacked as though the reason for the war was still fresh,
and their anger was no less fierce because of the long time-gap. Minds
would be less inflamed for battle

iussa, tube, promissa, preces. asperrima cernas 400
bella geri. non precipites telluris hiatus,
non undas timuere viri; sibi quisque videri
dux aliis milesque sibi. pars cratibus instat
continuas molita vias vallemque profundam
molibus iniectis vincunt; pars aspera clivi 405
impatiens hesisse subit. iam copia muri,
iam silices laxare licet, sed desuper urgent
Dardanide, incussasque trabes et saxea volvunt
fragmina; pars iaculis audax, pars aspera flammis
flagrantes invergit aquas. septum arbore Dimus 410
affectabat iter, fixoque in menia vultu,
heserat; hunc latices decalvavere profusi,
fulmineique imbres, nudum spoliatur utroque
crine caput penetratque fluens in viscera vulnus.
at testudineo Telamon defensus amictu 415
occultum furatur iter silicumque tenorem
ere domat iamque in preceps pendente ruina
cedit et effracta tandem prior urbe potitur.

Interfectio Laomedontis

Interea flammis populari vela parantem
percellit vox dira ducem: 'Cui, strenue ductor 420
Dardanidum, cui bella geris? civesne perosus
monstripari pacem pelagi sancire laboras
an pavidis profugisque instas, et, ne qua superstes
sit fuga, consumis classes? propioribus ausis

by orders, trumpets, promises or entreaties. The battles you can see being fought are extremely fierce. The Greek warriors had no fear of the steep sides of the moat nor the water in it. Each man seems to think of himself as a leader for the others and a soldier for himself. Some press on with wooden platforms, making a direct assault, filling the deep moat with huge boulders; others, not brooking delay, climb the steep side of the moat. Now they can attack the mass of the wall by pulling out the stones, but the Trojans attack them from above, tipping over them bits of rock and fractured timbers. Some throw their spears bravely while others cruelly pour down boiling water. Dimus was trying a path protected by a tree, and he hesitated with his eyes fixed on the walls. The mass of hot water showering down balded him, scalding the hair and beard from his unhelmeted head. The wounding flow penetrates into his entrails. But Telamon, covered by the tortoise formation, sneaks up stealthily and overcomes the hard resistance of the stones with his iron bar. And now, with the ruined wall about to fall headlong, he steps back, but he is the first to take possession of the city when it is finally broken into.

The Killing of Laomedon

Meanwhile a grim voice rocks the leader Laomedon as he prepares to destroy the ships with fire. 'On whose behalf are you fighting, great leader? Do you detest your fellow-citizens so much that you struggle to impose peace on the monster-bearing sea? Or are you attacking frightened runaways and burning the fleet so that no flight is possible for them?

intendere manus hostes, huc lumina flecte 425
atque urbem miserare tuam!' vix credulus heret
Laomedon cernitque tamen iam Pergama rumpi,
stare hostes, nutare Friges. rapit ocius agmen
attonitum bellique rudis non colligit alas,
sed sparsis properat signis. quem prepete gaudens 430
excipit occursu Tirynthius 'his'que ait 'olim
cum premerent portus optataque litora fessi,
exilem telluris opem tenuemque negasti,
seve, moram spreta pacis cum fronde Minerva.
sume vices: rediit hostis qui venerat hospes.' 435
sic fatur strictoque ducem transverberat ense
thoracisque moras clipeique umbramina raptim
dissipat atque animam tot defensoribus usam
elicit et Stygios iubet irrupisse Penates.
fit fuga Dardanidum mactato principe. at hostis 440
civiles predatur opes; pars cedibus iras
innumeris explere sitit. vox regia tandem
castigat rapidos Danao grassante tumultus.

'Parcite, victores Danai, compescite dextras!
labe pari peccat, pariter crudelis uterque, 445
qui cunctis parcit et nulli. nobilis ire est
citra iram punire reos. iam copia regni,
urbs cecidit, cessit hostis; cesoque tiranno
ut miseris faciles Graiorum exempla secuti
esse Friges discant, damus ultro rura colono, 450

The enemy troops are straining to perform daring deeds close at hand. Look this way and take pity on your city!' Laomedon stops, hardly able to believe it yet perceives that Troy is breached, the enemy is winning, the Trojans falling. He quickly recalls his astonished battle-force and hurries off with his troops all over the place, since he did not draw up the raw soldiers in battle formation. Tirynthian Hercules happily runs out to meet him at full speed. 'There was a time', he says, 'when you refused merely permission for a short stopover on your soil to those people who arrived on the longed-for beach of this harbour when they were tired out. You cruel savage, you ignored Minerva's olive branch of peace. Now pay the price: he who came as a guest now returns as an enemy.' Speaking thus he draws his sword and runs Laomedon through, forcing a way through the protective breastplate and covering shield. Thus drawing out his soul that was employing so many defensive layers, he orders it to descend to a home in hell. After the death of their king the Trojans flee. But their enemy loots the wealth of the city, some longing to satisfy their anger by indiscriminate slaughter. At last a kingly voice reprimands the rioting hordes of angry Greeks:

'Victorious Greeks, stop and check your right hands! Both are equally sinful and equally cruel whether they spare everybody or nobody. It is noble anger to punish the guilty without anger. Already the power of the kingdom as well as the city have fallen while the enemy has fled. With the death of the tyrant let the Trojans learn how to show pity for the unfortunate, following the example of the Greeks. We are happy to hand over the fields to the farmer,

castra viris, pontum nautis et civibus urbem.
at pereat, dira si quis de stirpe superstes,
hanc quoniam delere iuvat.' sic fatur, et ecce
Amphitus, Isiphilus, Volcontus et inclita vultu
Hesione sevis vincti post terga catenis 455
traduntur ducibus. hii dira in funera rapti,
hec, Telamon, tibi preda datur, quod Pergama victor,
quod prior effractam facilem das hostibus urbem.
ilicet Argolici preda Hesioneque potiti
incumbunt pelago laurumque, insigne triumphi, 460
puppibus exponunt penetrantque ad sidera plausu.

Reditus Priami ab orientali Frigia

His aberat Priamus aliam servatus in iram
fatorum casusque alios. cui Marte secundo
Eoos populata Friges victoria leta
faverat et reduci comites plausere triumphi. 465
dura hominum Lachesis! sors perfida! luditur anceps
imperium. Priamus natales ampliat agros,
Troia ruit; sceptroque novus dum queritur orbis,
sceptri nutat honos; faustos in regna meatus
fata dabant reduci, sed dira, sed aspera donis 470
invidit Fortuna suis, que, cum ardua donet,
gustatos graviore favos ulciscitur ira.
iamque urbis trepido conspectum pectore ductor
hauserat, occurrit luctus visumque salutat
e muris manuum plausus lacrimabilis. horror 475
adgreditur turbatque ducem totamque pererrat

the camp to the soldiers, the sea to the sailors and the city
to the citizens. But if any of this cruel line remains, let him
perish, since it is a public utility to wipe it out.' Thus he
speaks, and see, Amphitus, Isiphilus, Volcontus and Hesione whose
455 looks are famous are handed over to the Greek generals with their
hands chained behind their backs. The males are put to death cruelly
while Hesione is given to Telamon as a prize because he is the victor of
Pergamum, the first to have broken into the city and made it easy for the
enemy to take it. Immediately the Greeks set sail, taking with them
460 booty and Hesione while decking their ships with laurel, the sign of
victory. Their shouts reach the sky.

Return of Priam from Eastern Phrygia

Priam had been absent from this war, preserved for other misfortunes
and a different wrath of the fates. Joyous victory had blessed him
465 with a successful campaign to ravage Eastern Phrygia and his comrades
applauded him on his triumphal return. O harsh fates of men!
O perfidious chance! His double empire is mocked. Priam increases his
native lands while Troy itself falls. While new territory is sought
for his rule the glory of that rule is tottering. The fates were
70 giving him a successful return journey to his kingdom but cruel, harsh
chance begrudges him her gifts. Although she grants the heights she
then takes an even angrier revenge on those who have tasted honey.
Already the prince had taken in the sight of the city with trembling
heart when grief comes out to meet him. Sad beating of hands greets
75 him from the walls when he has been perceived. Horror invests the
prince, throwing him into confusion.

infelix planctus aciem. stant undique cives
solanturque suam Priamo spirante ruinam.
ille autem, licet interno compluta dolore
corda gemant, vultu lacrimas castigat adultas 480
ut saltem speret ducis ad solacia vulgus.
nam summe miser est cui nec sperare relictum est.

Descriptio Troie

Nec mora, diffusam spatiis maioribus urbem
integrat, ac potior constructio barbara Grecam
excludit themesim. medicati vulnera muri 485
respirant meliore manu, contentaque moles
in senum patuisse aditum et, qua saxa recedunt,
continuant valve duplices; hec cardine laxo
alternos pandit aditus, hec robur acernum
pectine ferrato tacitos suspendit in usus. 490
iamque arces cecidisse iuvat, iam machina maior
et lucro iactura fuit. muralia primas
propulsura manus pinnarum culmine denso
conspicuos tollunt apices, nec menia munit
rarior excubias turris factura secundas. 495
celsior in superas contendens vertice nubes
Ylios equaret gemini discrimina mundi.
si spacio contenta suo minus improba celo
parceret atque alium iam non presumeret orbem!
si Flegram conferre velis, si virginis arces 500
Assirie, feret hec potius discrimina lingue,
tela Iovis. nulli spaciosior ethere tractus

An unhappy lament runs through the whole army. The citizens stand around everywhere and find their consolation in Priam who is still alive. Although his heart inside him is flooded with grief, he
480 checks back the tears that welled up in his eyes so that his people could at least hope for some solace in their leader. For the most wretched person is one to whom no hope is left.

Description of Troy

Immediately Priam rebuilds the city, extending it over a greater surface area. A stronger Trojan construction shuts out Greek
485 retribution. The damage to the wall had been repaired to make it better than before, and the wall extended to allow six entrances. Where the blocks end twin gates continue; one opens both ways on
490 its turning hinge, the other contains a strong maplewood portcullis hidden in its top for use in war. By now the Trojans were glad their battlements had fallen for the construction was now bigger and so the loss was really a gain. The new walls would deter the first bands of attackers by their conspicuous height and tight
495 crenellations. Towers are no less frequent to provide efficient watchpoints for defending the walls. The palace Ylios rises higher, soaring into the upper clouds, and would reach the dividing line between the lower and upper atmosphere if it were content with its space; if, less ambitiously, it respected the upper air and did
500 not presume to occupy another world! If you wished to compare Phlegra or the other citadels of the Assyrian virgin, this tower would rather deserve the division of languages or the thunderbolts of Jupiter. To no other has a larger tract in the upper air been allowed

contigit aut tantum paciens indulsit Olimpus.
pene pares totam turres sparguntur in urbem
Ciclopum fasse studium, civisque superbus 505
celsa petens fastidit humum. surgentia passim
exalant piceas incensa piralia flammas.
ingenti Ucalegon consumens aera tecto
arduus alta tenet, Antenor menibus equis
certat. at inconstans nunc maior nunc minor egris 510
Anchises parcit pedibus gressumque perosus
e speculis videt urbis opes plaususque viarum.

Haut procul incumbens urbi mediantibus arvis
Ydeus consurgit apex. vetus incola montis,
silva, viret: vernat abies procera, cupressus 515
flebilis, interpres laurus, vaga pinus, oliva
concilians, cornus venatrix, fraxinus audax,
stat comitis paciens ulmus nunquamque senescens
cantatrix buxus. paulo proclivius arvum
ebria vitis habet et dedignata latere 520
Cancricolam poscit Phebum. vicinus aristas
pregnantes fecundat ager. non plura Falernus
vina bibit, non tot pascit Campania messes.

Proxima rura rigans alio peregrinat ab orbe
visurus Troiam Simois longoque meatu 525
emeruisse velit ut per tot regna, tot urbes,
exeat equoreas tandem Troianus in undas.
Dumque indefesso miratur Pergama visu,

or patient Olympus been so indulgent. Towers almost as high are scattered throughout the whole city, testifying to the toil of the
505 Cyclops. The arrogant citizen despises the ground as he seeks the heights. Chimneys rising everywhere belch out their smoky flames when lit. Using up the air with his huge building Ucalegon has a steeply towering house while Antenor rivals him with walls rising equally
510 high. But limping Anchises, who hates walking, spares his crippled feet, merely looking out from his vantage point at the prosperity of the city's crowded streets.

Not far off, on the other side of some fields, the summit of Mount Ida
515 rises, leaning towards the city. The wood that had long been there was flourishing: the tall fir, the sad cypress. the prophetic laurel, the travelling pine, the conciliatory olive, the hunting cornel and the bold ash grew there, while the elm, supporting its companion, and the evergreen musical boxwood also stand there. The drunken vine
520 occupies the slightly steeper terrain. Scorning to seek shelter it demands the burning sun. A neighbouring field enriches the swelling ears of corn. Falernus does not produce more wine nor does Campania so many harvests.

The river Simois irrigates nearby countryside as it travels from
525 another world to see Troy. By its long journey through so many kingdoms and cities it would like to have earned the right to flow out into the sea finally as a Trojan river. And while it gazes in unending amazement at Troy

lapsurum suspendit iter fluviumque moratur
tardior et totam complecti destinat urbem. 530
suspensis infensus aquis violentior instat
Nereus atque amnem cogens procul ire minorem
proximus accedit urbi. contendere credas
quis propior, sic alternis concurritur undis,
sic crebras iterant voces, sic iurgia miscent. 535

Undique siderei maiestas conflua mundi
Yliacum dignata solum iuga, menia, pontum
vestit et astrifero dat respiramina collo.
Ydeos Cibele colles colit, ipsa superbis
regnatura iugis reliquos tibi, Delia, saltus 540
donat et Ydeis pensat venatibus orbem.
pampineum te, Bacche, nemus, te spicea cingit
silva, Ceres. Neptunus aquas, navalia Phebus,
arces Pallas habet et habetur Pallade fatum.
est sacer urbe locus media modicumque laborat 545
in cumulum pigmeus apex, quem surgere plene,
quem plane residere neges. hic celsa superbi
fulgurat ara Iovis non sceptro et fulmine nudi,
non qualem Tirius, non qualem predicat Indus.

it delays its faltering course, slows down its already sluggish
30 flow, and causes the whole city to be encircled. The sea is
angry at the delay to its waters and presses in more violently,
forcing the smaller river to move away so that it can get right
up to the city. You would think they were striving to see who
35 could get closer, such was the meeting of the two currents, such
the continual roaring of the mutual strife.

From everywhere the majestic gods of the starry sphere converge,
finding the Trojan land worthy, investing the mountains, the walls
and the sea. Thus they gave respite to the heaven-bearing neck of
40 Atlas. Cybele inhabits the hills of Ida with the intention of
ruling on the lofty peaks while she allots the rest of the groves
to you, Diana, and determines the area to be available for the
hunts on Ida. The vine-forest houses you, Bacchus, while a
cornfield is your home, Ceres. Neptune occupies the sea, Apollo
the harbour, Pallas the citadel. The fate of the city is held
45 by Pallas. In the middle of the city is a sacred spot where a
tiny promontory struggles to reach a mediocre height which one
would describe as not rising fully nor lying quite flat. Here
gleams a high altar to proud Jupiter, possessing his sceptre
and thunderbolt, not like the one the Tyrian or the Indian
worships.

Liber secundus de iudicio Paridis

Iam floret Priamus populoso pignore felix,
felix coniugio, felix natalibus arvis,
si superi, si fata sinant, si stare beatis
permissum. videt Allecto quas fregerat arces
fortuna meliore frui; videt, ardet et idris 5
irascens circumque genas et tempora crebris,
'Mene' inquit 'reginam Herebi mundique potentem
atque utinam celi, regnum mortale lacesset
eternum? pudet heu, lascivit Troia superstes
post Danaos, quibus usa fui. nostrisne triumphis 10
contendit vincique negat? ruat ocius ergo
a cunis concessa mihi!' sic questa, quietem
invidet exiguam Priamo raptumque sororis
servilemque colum et lacrimas obiectat inultas.

O hominum superumque pater! si numina curas, 15
cur hominem plectis? miserene quod incola terre
despicitur? certe lacrimis noctique dedisti
proscriptas a luce animas. pater optime,
tandem flectere, redde polo reduces vel funera saltem
exilii tutare tui! cur impia sevit 20
Allecto in miseros? cur Pergama dia fatigat
tot superis confisa suis? tolle, inclita, tolle,
virgo, moras nec passa premi, quas incolis, arces
Gorgone pretenta Stigias perstringe Medusas!
en aras, en thura sibi communia poscunt 25

Second Book - The Judgement of Paris

Priam is now flourishing, blessed with numerous children, blessed in marriage, blessed in his native kingdom, if only the gods and the fates were to allow it, or indeed it if was permissible to remain blessed. Allecto sees the defences she had broken enjoy a better fortune. She sees, she is inflamed and rages with many snakes around her cheeks and temples. 'Will an earthly kingdom', she says, 'always provoke me, the powerful queen of hell and earth, and one day, I hope, of heaven too? What shame is mine! Troy is still standing, provocatively prosperous after the defeat by the Greeks who were my agents. Does Troy put my triumph in question and refuse to admit defeat? May it collapse quickly, this city that was placed in my power at its very foundation!' Complaining like this she begrudges Priam even a minimal respite, reminding him of his sister's abduction, her servile fate and her unavenged tears.

O father of the gods and men! If you look after the deities why do you punish mankind? Is he looked down on because he lives on this wretched earth? In truth, you have abandoned to tears and darkness the souls that have been exiled from your light. Best of fathers, yield at last, return and restore the souls to heaven, or at least protect the dead victims of the exile you imposed! Why does evil Allecto act cruelly against the unfortunate? Why does she harass holy Pergamum that puts its trust in its numerous gods? O famous virgin, do not delay. Do not allow the citadels you inhabit to be assailed. With the Gorgon's head in front of you turn to stone those Stygian Medusas! See, they demand that your altars and incense should be shared with them

nutrices scelerum Furie noctisque tirannos
exorare iubent. celum intra menia clausum,
concives habuisse deos haut linquet inultum
Thesiphone regique suo cultore negato,
quam dedit, invidiam Frigius luet. ecce profundis 30
curarum furiis vigilique impulsa dolore
mens Priamum in diversa trahit: nunc Marte reposcit
Hesionem, nunc bella timet. sententia tandem
certior inniti precibus, temptare Pelasgos
blandiciis. voce hac legatum Anthenora demum 35
instruit et parvo claudit mandata libello.

'Hactenus, invicti gens imperiosa Pelasgi,
libertas Asie nullis concussa vigebat
casibus. invidit solitum fortuna favorem
et rerum decrevit apex. verum Hercule vinci 40
turpe minus tantoque leves auctore ruine.
nunc, quia conciliat humiles favor, exuo regem,
in miseras descendo preces. sic India Bachum,
sic Cirrum Cresus, Thamirim sic, Cire, rogabas.
at si Parca prior qua ceperat ire mearet, 45
ipse orandus eram geminumque impensus in usum
aut pacem regerem iudex aut prelia princeps.
proh superi, que dira orbem deludit Erinis!
exieram miles, tractabam prelia ductor,
victor eram. sed quid Eoo blanda triumpho, 50
si mestos leto reditus, Fortuna, parabas?
heccine post tantos mihi debita pompa labores?

those fomentors of crime, the Furies. They even give instructions to pray to the tyrants of hell. Tisiphone will not leave unavenged the fact that heavenly gods are enclosed within the walls of Troy and are fellow-citizens of the Trojans, and because Priam refused to worship her king, Pluto, he will pay for the ill-will he created. Lo, driven by the deep anger of his worries and his keen grief, Priam's mind is torn in two directions: now he demands Hesione's return by force, now he is afraid of force. At last his considered thought is to rely on entreaty, to use flattery on the Greeks. Ultimately he instructed Antenor as his ambassador with these words and conveyed his orders in a short letter:

'Until now, o mighty nation of unconquered Greeks, the liberty of Asia flourished with no misfortunes to shake it. Then Fortune begrudged us her normal favour and our supremacy declined. But actually defeat by Hercules is not a great disgrace, and destruction wrought by such a great man is bearable. Now because humility induces favour, I put my royal honour to one side and stoop to humble entreaty. Thus India pleaded with Bacchus, Croesus with Cyrus, and you, Cyrus, with Thamiris. But if my previous fate had continued on its course, I would have been the subject of entreaties. Employed in a twofold purpose I would have acted as a presiding judge in peace and as a general in war. O gods above, what a cruel curse mocks the world! I left my country as a soldier, I fought battles as a general and I was victorious. But, Fortune, why were you preparing a return saddened by death when you had made me happy with an eastern triumph? Was this the pomp that was due to me after such a great struggle?

sic merui tibi, Troia, dari? que leta parabas
cum redii! seva illa dies semperque gemenda
qua reduci primum patrie mestissima clades 55
visa, audita simul! melius, quem fecimus, hostis,
aut cui factus eram, vitam hanc tot tristia passam
rupisset gladio. sceptrone et culmine regni
dulce frui sic, sic fratrum patrisque perempti,
sic rapte memor Hesiones? miserescite, magni 60
Mirmidonum proceres! cesum lugere parentem,
exhaustam vidisse domum lapsosque Penates
sit satis: Hesionem lacrimis solatia tantis
reddite! parva quidem posco, sed muneris instar
maioris; vite pariter pariterque saluti 65
exanimem dabitis,' sic postquam questus, et ipsi
et cui carta datur tepidus fluit imber in ora.

Anthenor, Zephiris blandum spondentibus equor,
haurit iter rapiensque ducis mandata per undas
Magnesii fines Sparten pretervolat altam 70
fatidicamque Pilon. paucis ubi tracta diebus
ocia dequestus cedit; non Pelea magnum,
Tindaridas geminos, Piliam flexere senectam
verba ducis. leti tandem Thelamonis ad urbem
flectit iter Lachesisque fugam vestigat in omnes. 75

Nuptie Hesiones

Regia celsa nitet complutaque murice multo
purpura Sidonios dispergit in atria luxus

Was this how I deserved to return to you, Troy? What happy events you were preparing for my return! That was a cruel day to be lamented forever, a day on which the most pitiful destruction of my homeland first met my eyes and ears as I returned. It would have been better if the enemy I made or for whom I was made had put an end with the sword to this life of mine which had suffered so much sadness. Is it a pleasure for me to hold the sceptre of royal power like this, when I remember my brothers and dead father, and my abducted sister Hesione? Show pity, great leaders of the Mirmidons! Let it be enough to have mourned a slaughtered parent, to have seen one's family wiped out, one's home destroyed! Return Hesione to me as a consolation for such great mourning! I am not asking much, but nevertheless it would be like a great gift to me. You will be giving both life and health to a dead man.' After this complaint a warm stream of tears rolls down both Priam's face and Antenor's, the recipient of the letter.

When the west winds promise a calm sea Antenor sets sail, carrying the king's letter over the waves. He speeds across the land of Magnesia, towering Sparta and prophetic Pylos. After a few days in each he leaves, complaining bitterly about wasting his time. The king's words had no influence on mighty Peleus or on the twin sons of Tyndareus or on the old man of Pylos. Finally Antenor moves on to the city of Telamon the happy, with Lachesis looking for a way out for all concerned.

Hesione's Wedding

The tall palace gleams, and purple dye from many purple-fish spreads Tyrian ostentation over the rooms,

sollempnem confessa diem, qua iungit herilem
Iuno thorum. leto cuncti convivia plausu
concelebrant, populoque suo certamina prima 80
ventripotens ponit genius, cenare decorum
et mensas variare iuvat. nec pocula desunt
fecundam factura sitim, repetisse voluptas,
et vites conferre libet. civiliter ipsi
indulgent proceres ciathis; bibulique clientes 85
'Heus, Hymenee!' sonant et in aurea pocula fusi
invitant sese pateris. plebs mixta - Britanni
certatura siti longique potentior haustus -
plebeos gaudet calices et sobria vina
regali mutasse mero, redimitque voluptas 90
rara moras nec cessat hians dum pectore victo
lingua fluat, crescant lichni, vestigia nutent.
cetera multiplici lascivit curia plausu:
pars sistris, pars grata liris, pars ore canoro
nativas ostentat opes contentaque nervis 95
arterie non artis opem, non carmina nervi
ad vocis mendicat opus. se quelibet ornat
musa libens, qua voce placet, qua dote superbit.
non tamen indulgent studiis communibus omnes,
etatum parium similis concordia, narrat 100
cum sene canicies, ludit cum pube iuventus.
at modulii alternat libamina prima coraules
previus et dociles hoc explicat ore choreas:
'Plaudite, concives, Salamine ditis alumpni,
plaudite! victori nubit Priameia nostro 105

announcing the festive day on which Juno makes the royal bed conjugal.
Everyone with happy applause celebrates the wedding feast while the
Genius of the Powerful Appetite sets his first contests for his people:
it is a pleasure to be at table, a pleasure to have several courses.
Nor are the drinks missing that create an abundant thirst; here the
pleasure is to go back for more and to compare the different wines.
The nobles themselves in the manner of townspeople drink heavily
while their thirsty vassals shout 'Hail, Hymen!', and having been
generous with the golden cups now drink their own health from bowls.
The drunken lower class, forerunners of the Britons for their thirst,
and more competent in drinking deep, are happy to have changed their
common cups and ordinary wines for a royal vintage. This rare joy
for them makes up for any slowness in the service, and their ever-
open mouths do not admit defeat until, with their minds blown, their
tongues lose their power, the candles seem double and their steps
totter. The rest of the court enjoy themselves with many a different
noise: some delight with their castanets, some with lyres, while others
show their natural talents in tuneful song. Content with their vocal
chords they did not beg for the help of art or for the sounds of a
stringed instrument to back up their voices. Each singer gladly goes
on show with the voice that gives pleasure, the gift he is proud of.
But not everyone indulges in the communal pleasures: the different
generations go their own ways. The white-haired chat with the old
while the young men joke together. A musician comes forward, directs
the first movements of the dance and arranges the listening dancers
in position, saying: 'Fellow citizens, inhabitants of rich Salamis,
clap your hands! Hesione, sister of Priam, is marrying our hero.'

Hesione.' clamant una 'Feliciter!' omnes
congeminantque iterum 'Feliciter!' ille canoros
concilians in plectra modos his exit in aures:

'Quid gentis Danae proavos, quid prisca stupemus
prelia? miremur potius, quem protulit etas, 110
qua fruimur, rerum patrem mundique patronum
Amphitroniadem, axis quem laudat uterque;
cuius opem sevos debellatura Gigantes
astra petunt geminoque armari fulmine poscunt.
hunc non Iuno ferox, non accusator iniquus, 115
non labor exhausit. redolent cunabula primum
vix orte virtutis opus: Nemeus adultos
expavit terror humeros; Erimanthus abacto
respiravit apro; victricis victima clave
absolvit Cretem taurus; dux flebat Hiberus 120
damnatis quas Cacus opes absconderat antris;
non angues Lerne reduces, non Cerberus ingens,
non Laphite domuere virum; vigilata draconi
poma tulit; pestem Libicam libravit in auras
edocuitque hostem nocituris artibus astra, 125
qui quondam geometer erat; Achelous in armis,
Nessus in effugio nimis exarsisse queruntur;
Otrisios mactavit equos, revocavit ab armis
Ypoliten domuitque fero Stimphalides arcu.
nec solum tibi se tellus, sed sidera debent; 130
vector eras et vector eris. da, maxime, felix
auspicium, letum tribuas nubentibus omen

They all shout in unison 'Good luck', repeating it again and again.
Adapting the beautiful rhythms to his lyre, the musician addresses
all of them:

'Why do we marvel at the ancestors of the Greek nation and their
10 earliest battles? Rather let us admire the one our present age has
brought forth, the father of our existence, the protector of the world,
Hercules son of Amphitryon, whom the whole world praises. It was
his help the heavens sought when they were able to fight the savage
Giants, calling for the armed presence of those twin thunderbolts,
15 Jupiter and Hercules. Neither fierce Juno nor the evil accuser
Eurystheus, nor his labours sapped his strength. His cradle indicated
the first exploit of a new-born hero: the scourge of Nemea trembled
in fear at the sight of his shoulders when he was full grown. Mount
20 Erymanthus breathed again when the boar had been put to flight. He
freed Crete from the bull that became a victim of his victorious club.
The Spanish chief, Geryon, wept for his cattle which Cacus then hid in
his doomed cave. Neither the self-renewing heads of the Hydra, nor
huge Cerberus, nor the Lapiths could tame the man. He took the apples
watched over by the dragon. He held aloft Antaeus, the scourge of Libya,
25 and by means of his skills that were to prove injurious he taught his
enemy about the stars - beforehand Antaeus was only a geometrician.
Achelous in fighting and Nessus in absconding had learned to their
cost about his excessive love for Deianira. He slaughtered the
horses of Diomedes, he made Hippolyte forget fighting and tamed the
30 Stymphalians with his savage bow. Not only is the earth in your debt,
but the heavens too. You were a carrier and you will be carried.
O great one, give a favourable auspice, grant a happy omen to the
bridal pair

et prosit cecinisse tibi. si iusseris, ibunt
monstra procul, ridebit Hymen Iunoque favebit
iam tua. sic Hebe pariat Saturnia celo 135
et nostro nova nupta duci.' plaudentia rursus
tecta sonant festoque favet plebs leta tumultu.
sola tamen duro turbat convivia vultu
Hesione. spernit plausus oditque faventes
nil titulis permota suis, non dote superba, 140
non cultus mirata novos. sibi rapta videri,
mesta queri et quociens sibi plaudit regia nomen
regine, captiva pavet nec libera fidit,
sed iussa in thalamos timide ventura coactos.
cumque aliis modulentur aves, que coniuga fata 145
exhilarant meliore lira, sibi credula fingit
noctivagas ululasse striges, bubone sinistro
tecta premi Stigioque satas Acheronte sorores
funestas gessisse faces, heu, ceca futuri,
quam sevum patriis paritura nepotibus hostem! 150
quin etiam oblatos calices, oblata recusat
cimbia, nunc tacito perfundit pocula luctu
et lacrimas bibit ipsa suas segnique morantes
crescentesque cibos gustu ieiuna fatigat.

Tristior interea Frigius delabitur hospes 155
in portus, Salamina, tuos ramoque verendus
Palladio celsas subit arces. cetera nosse
curia cunctatur, concivem sola Frigemque
agnoscit nova nupta virum pudibundaque vultum
flectit et orantem miratur talibus illum: 160

and may our song to you be to our advantage. If you give the
order the evil spirits will go away, Hymen will smile and Juno,
35 now on your side, will grant her approval. May Hebe, daughter of
Juno, give birth in heaven and may the new bride produce offspring
for our king.' The sound of applause goes through the palace again
while the joyous population joins in the noisy celebrations. Only
Hesione upsets the festivities with her unsmiling face. She scorns
40 the applause and hates the well-wishers, unmoved by her new position
or marvellous dowry and unimpressed by her new life-style. She thinks
of herself as abducted. She complains sadly, and each time the
palace applauds her title as queen she fears for herself as a captive,
not trusting in her freedom, but going into a forced marriage afraid
45 and under duress. And although birds that add to the charm of a
wedding ceremony with their lovely song sing to the others, Hesione
thinks and even believes that night-flying owls had screeched, that
the sinister horned owl is sitting on the roof, that the sisters born
in Stygian Acheron had shaken their deadly torches. Alas, unaware of
50 the future, she will bring forth a savage enemy for her father's
descendants! She even refuses the goblets and the drinking vessels
offered but fills her cup with silent grief, drinking her own tears
while her lack of appetite and slow eating cause the waiting piles of
food to grow.

55 Meanwhile, a sadder, Trojan guest slips into your harbour, Salamis,
and enters the lofty palace with Pallas' olive branch to afford him
respect. The rest of the palace is slow to discover his identity -
only the new bride recognises the man as a fellow Trojan, and
60 shamefacedly she turns away yet admiring him as he makes this plea:

'Inclita sceptrigeri proles Iovis et minus uno
in natum perducte gradu, reverende Pelasgis
iustitia belloque potens, tibi supplicat omnis
cum duce Troia suo, Thelamon. miserescite, cives,
tuque prior, non tot terraque marique labores 165
incassum fluxisse sinas! post aspera multa
huc tandem, huc veni. cerno quam querere iussus.
Hesionem cerno. non hec commercia certe
Iuno probat; victore suo captiva fruetur,
flens hilari, famulans domino vel barbara Greco? 170
redde magis: tot vestra nurus Europa superbas,
tot celebres habet illa faces. melioribus ortam
quere aliam fatis: hec edita sidere diro
in raptus damnata fuit facilisque vel omni
preda venit, semperque suis rapienda minatur. 175
noverat Argolicas Alcides, noverat alter
cum Polluce error, novit cum Nestore Peleus,
cum levis assensu facili tibi preda daretur
Hesione; meque haut fines trusisset in istos
infelix Priamus, si quid de gente superstes 180
cognata patrie pensaret damna ruine.
hanc tibi, non superis, animam debere fatetur
quam sibi servatam gaudet.' 'sibi? sed "Telamoni"
dic potius,' subicit Telamon invitaque flentis
oscula predatur et 'in hos' ait 'ire lacertos 185
emerui gladio.' sic interfatur et illud
Dirceum memorat: 'teneo longumque tenebo.'

'Famous offspring of ruling Jupiter, brought into this life at only one remove from him, powerful in war and revered by the Greeks for your fairness, Telamon, the whole of Troy with its king implores you. O citizens, but particularly you, Telamon,
65 show pity. Do not permit so many tribulations on land and sea to have been suffered in vain. After so much hardship it is to here that I have finally come. I see the one I have orders to seek; I see Hesione. Juno certainly does not approve of this
70 wedding. Will a captive find pleasure from her captor, will a mourner from one who is happy, a servant from her master or a barbarian from a Greek? Give her back, instead. Your Europe has so many aristocratic young women, so many reputable brides. Seek one who was born under a luckier star. Hesione was born under a cruel sign, destined to be abducted. She comes as an
75 easy prey for anyone and is always under threat of being abducted from her companions. Hercules had Greek women, as did the identical twins, Castor and Pollux. Peleus and Nestor still had theirs when Hesione was readily given to you as unimportant booty. And unhappy
80 Priam would not have bundled me off to these lands if some survivor of his family remained to compensate for the loss of his fatherland that was ravaged. He admits that she owes her life to you, not to the gods, and he is happy that she has been kept alive for him.'
'For him? For Telamon, you mean', says Telamon, snatching unwelcome
85 kisses from the weeping Hesione. 'I earned by my sword the right to enjoy her embraces.' Thus he interrupts and recalls the Theban saying: 'I hold it and will do so for a long time.'

Pulsus abit Frigius relegensque quod hauserat equor
in patrios delatus agros iter explicat omne
civibus, Hesiones talamos et nulla Pelasgos 190
iura sequi, bellumque hortatur. at eger iniqua
suspicione Paris: 'ne credite; ludimur', inquit,
'Dardanide! miror hilarem. sibi commodus uni.
non sperata refert, non quod commune decorum
molitus speciale bonum. male publica curat 195
qui sua pluris habet; gelidoque haut utitur ense
saucia proximitas. mihi classem ac vela parate.
ibo, ibo: non me, pavidus quas obicit Hector,
terruerint Sirtes, non arma adversa vel hostes;
non aditus in regna graves. mihi numen ab alto 200
indulget dictatque vias spemque addit ituro.
mira quidem, sed vera, duces, advertite, pandam.

Somnium Paridis

Desertura virum flebat Pallantias ortum
processisse diem, sed iam maturior estus
solverat algentes lacrimas; me dulce trahebat 205
certamen nemorum populari lustra, fugaces
indagare feras facilique instare molosso.
ocius exciti qui casse vel ore vel aure,
fraude, sono, sensu, ludentes prelia, casse
fallunt, ore cient, vestigant aure, simulque 210
invadunt saltus. me nutu numinis error
devius in spatium seductius, in nemus altum
egit venarique dedit secreta dearum.

Antenor leaves rebuffed, returns over the sea he had previously crossed. Having reached home he recounts the whole journey to the citizens, the wedding of Hesione and the Greeks' disregard of rights. He recommends war. But Paris, troubled by unjust suspicions, says: 'Don't believe him, Trojans. We are being tricked. I marvel at his happiness. He has worked only for his own good. He has not brought back what we hoped for, has not striven for that special goal of common good. He who places personal wealth first is a bad upholder of public interests. When a blood-relative has been injured one takes revenge with an uncowardly sword. Prepare a fleet for me to set sail. I shall go. The Syrtes that frightened Hector puts forward as an obstacle will not scare me. Nor do armed enemies facing me. Nor even the difficulties involved in entering the kingdoms of the Greeks. A heavenly power looks kindly on me, indicates the way and gives me hope for my journey. Leaders, listen to me as I recount something that is fantastic but true.

The Dream of Paris

Aurora, descendant of the giant Pallas, about to leave her husband's bed, was weeping that the day had begun to be set in motion, but by now an increasing heat had made her cold tears disappear. The pleasant sport of the woods was enticing me to plunder the dens of wild animals, to pursue them in flight and to track them down with the easily-trained dogs. Quickly stirred into action are those who with net, voice or ear, by trickery, noise or flair, play at war - that is, the trappers, the beaters and the trackers enter the woods together. Because of the will of a deity I wandered off course into a more remote part, deep in the woods, which allowed me to hunt the secrets of the goddesses.

Idei regina sinus dignissima Phebo
laurus inoffenso frondosum vertice crinem 215
explicat, et nemoris proscripta plebe minoris
sola viret, nullique suas communicat umbras.
cetera Cirream veneratur silva iuventam,
celsum submittens apicem, longeque reducta
maiorem temere poscentes aera frondes 220
castigat metuitque sacris occurrere ramis.
huc deus, aut casus, certe gratissimus error,
pertulit ereptum sociis. hac letus in umbra
mirabar laurum vivacis lege iuvente
nil Iove mutato passam: mirabar et Eurum 225
murmure adulantem foliis, et frondibus auram
secretum spirare suum; cum lanquida sensim
fur oculi somnus invitans ocia, blandum
pectoris elusit studium curasque fefellit.
sic caput herboso proiectum cespite fultus, 230
delicias hausi superum, nec frivola suetus
in plebem lusisse sopor sed somnia regum
dignatus subiit. magni mox nupta Tonantis
et Venus et Pallas sese languentibus ultro
ingessere oculis, quarum que maxima fando 235
vix bene maturam visa est solvisse quietem.

Conflictus dearum de preiudicio forme

Oratio Iunonis

'Venimus in saltus Frigios, O Dardane, veni
magni nupta Iovis, venit Mavortia Pallas,

A laurel tree, queen of the vale of Ida and most worthy of Apollo,
215 unfurls its leafy crown at an unrivalled height. It flourishes there on its own, as the crowd of lesser trees is far removed from it and it therefore sheds no shade on any other tree. The other trees in the wood revere the evergreen of Apollo, bowing their tall crests, and from a distance rebuke those leaves that
220 have the audacity to demand more sunlight. They are afraid of tangling with its sacred branches. It was to here that a deity or chance - certainly a very welcome diversion - led me away from my comrades. At ease in the shade, I admired the laurel that
225 suffered no change whatever the weather because it was an evergreen. I was admiring too the east wind caressing the leaves with its gentle breath, and the breeze whispering its secret to the branches, when sleep, robbing me of my sight, bade me rest my senses in repose. It playfully removed the pleasant pursuit of hunting from
230 my mind and cheated my intentions. Thus resting my head down on the grassy turf I experienced the delights of the gods. Sleep of the sort that graces the dreams of kings, not that which usually plays frivolous tricks on the lower classes, came to me. Immediately Juno, the wife of the great Thunder king, and Venus and Pallas
235 entered my tired eyes. The greatest of these seemed to put an end to my sleep almost before it had begun by saying:

The Goddesses' Arguments about the Beauty Contest

Juno's Speech

'We have come to the Phrygian woods, O Trojan, - that is, I the bride of great Jupiter have come, the warrior Pallas has come,

venit blanda Venus. gratare, en noster alumpnus,
quod dare Parca neget, timeat promittere votum, 240
sideree libram forme dedit. ipsa Tonantis
unica, que trini dispenso federa regni
cui parent unde Neptuni, Tartara Ditis,
astra Iovis, non si laudor censore caduco
indignor, non grata minus reditura Tonanti, 245
si nostro dubius hesit mortalis in ore.
quod longum est mirantis erit; neu forte putetur
mendax quem debet famulatrix fama favorem,
quod rarum superis, nudos en aspice vultus.
talis in amplexus venio Iovis. ergo quis ausus 250
Pallada Gorgoneam bellatricemque Medusam
hiis conferre genis? non sic pudor exulat omnis
ut populi terror, vulgi fuga, baiula leti,
quo terret, placuisse velit. vis, dira, doceri?
"diva" tamen dictura fui. non hic opus ense, 255
angues tolle tuos, armatos exue vultus,
da facilem visu faciem, frontem exere, cedat
cassis et inclusum sine respirare cerastam!
detege quod galea horrendum, quod parma pudendum
occulit atque aude preconia vera mereri! 260
hicne nitor calibis, hoc aurum hostile decoris
extorquebit opem? nescis, sevissima, nescis:
in calibe horror inest, in casside fulminat aurum,
in capulo crudescit ebur. sic docta minaces
delicias affert et vult placuisse Minerva. 265
tune Iovem mentita patrem? qua pelice nostra

seductive Venus has come. Be happy. Look, my beloved stepson
40 has given you what fate will not give and what your prayers fear
to conceive, namely the judgement of heavenly beauty. I, Jupiter's
only love, who administer the laws of the three kingdoms, to whom
the sea of Neptune obeys, as do Pluto's hell and Jupiter's heaven,
I will not get angry if I am judged by a mortal judge. I will not
45 return to Jupiter any less appreciated if a hesitant mortal takes
a long time to appreciate my beauty. If he does take time it will
be because he is lost in admiration. So that the favour which Fame,
my familiar, owes me, should not appear false, look at my uncovered
face - a sight rarely offered to the gods. I am like this when I
50 embrace Jupiter. So who would dare to compare Pallas the Gorgon,
the battling Medusa, with me for beauty? All sense of shame is not
exiled if the terror of the people, the router of the mob, the carrier
of death, should thus wish to seduce by the very quality that inspires
terror. Do you want a bit of advice, malevolent one? Sorry, I meant
55 to say "heavenly one". You won't need your sword here. Take off
your snakes and your armoured headgear. Let us see your face clearly.
Show us your forehead; off with your helmet now and let the horned
serpents that are under it have a breather! Reveal the horror that
60 the helmet hides, the disgrace that the shield hides, and be brave
enough to warrant a genuine evaluation! Will this gleam of steel
or this gold of your armour win for you the rich beauty prize? You
are wrong, most cruel one, you are wrong: there is horror in your
steel, the gold in your helmet has a baleful sheen, the ivory of your
65 sword-hilt flashes cruelly. Thus does learned Minerva bring along
her aggressive pleasures and she wants to be liked. Did you falsely
pretend that Jupiter was your father? By which of our whores

in luctus audente suos? sed matre carere
creditur. o superum pudor! hincne animosa superbit
solius meminisse viri dicique virago
emeruit? certe superos invisa fatigat, 270
mortales consumit. "at est Mavortia" dicunt -
ergo mares vorat. "at Pallas" - sit, sed quia pallet
vel quia Pallanti iugulum scidit. hinc color, inde
dextra nocens nomen alterno iure meretur.

Tuque, sed o facinus! tune, inquam, prodiga sexus, 275
femina plus quam iura sinant et mollior equo,
tune ergo, Venus, ausa venis in premia forme?
an nescis cui iura petis communia? sed quis
credet? tot Iuno similes habet? unica quondam
et nullis equanda fui! cum provida mundum 280
digereret Natura suum, sine coniuge coniunx
stabat et in florem vultu crescente severum
stabat adhuc cum sic mater Natura: "Quid heres,
celi heres? quod poscis habes: hec sanguine iuncta
iunctior amplexu. soror est, coniunx erit. una 285
e numero selecta tibi - una, sed unica, cuius
nec similem memoret tellus nec sidera norint.
absque pari parit illa tibi." sic fata negantem
in fratris cupidi dedit oscula. conscius ille
optati sceptrum tribuit commune sorori. 290
ergo eat et vultus nostros Ericina lacessat.
nuptum ivi selecta Iovi: sed fallitur. isset
diva Paphi pocius? quid ni? ortus nacta serenos

whose daring was to bring her grief? But they say she has no mother.
O shame of the gods! Is it for this reason she proudly boasts that
70 she keeps only man in mind and has deserved to be called a virago?
It is true - the hateful creature wearies the gods and consumes
mortals. "But she is Mavortian" people say - so she mauls men.
"But she is Pallas" - agreed, but either because she is pallid or
because she slit Pallas' throat. In one respect her complexion, in
another her murderous right hand, have given her a double right to her
name.

75 And you, Venus, you scandal! You, I say, you dispenser of sex, more
feminine than is lawful and more lewd than is right, are you daring
to come to this beauty contest? Don't you know whom you are measuring
yourself against? But who will believe it? Juno has so many equals?
80 Once I was unique and had no rivals! When provident Nature ordered
her world my husband had no wife, and when his face was beginning to
sprout a stern beard he was still without one, so Mother Nature said:
Why do you delay, heir to the heavens? You have what you are asking
85 for. She who is joined to you in blood will be joined even closer
in bed. She is your sister; she will be your wife. One chosen for
you from a number and yet one who is unique. Earth cannot recall and
the heavens do not know anyone like her. She will produce incomparable
children for you." Speaking thus, Nature handed me over against my
90 will to my brother's lustful embraces. He was aware of what he
wanted and shared his sceptre with his sister. So, let Sicilian
Venus go and challenge my beauty. I was selected to go and marry
Jupiter. But that is wrong - should the goddess of Paphos have gone
in my place? Why not? She had a pure birth,

concrevit spumante freto cesisque pudendis.
hec patrem factura Iovem, tibi bellice Mavors, 295
et populo pareret! hac anceps etheris heres
aurea degeneri violaret regna metallo,
quique nec indicio Phebi nec vindice textu
securam potuit noctemque fidemque mereri,
Lennius ultum iret alieni probra pudoris, 300
lenius et proprios non suspiraret amores.
ut Frigium sileam - quis vulgatissima nescit
furta dee? "Sed blanda, sed alma, sed aurea" - nectit
blanda dolos, alit alma malum, petit aurea donum.
olim, nam memini, certandi sola potestas 305
cum Iove nostra fuit. ubi tunc Venus? illane venit
tercia? ubi Pallas? an quarta, ut iussa, veniret?
Tiresia certe steterat sub iudice Iuno.
sed taceo. tu, Frix, potior tu disce mereri
Iunonem que sceptra ferat, que commodet aurum! 310
tot mundus miratur opes, tot regna comete
dispensant : que sceptra velis, quas, elige, terras.
quicquid agas, quocumque fluat sententia, nosti
Iunonem placuisse Iovi; Iunonie iudex,
censorem ne sperne Iovem!" sic alta profando 315
regine multum meminit vultumque superbum
vocibus ingessit contempta fronte precantis.

Prodit in aspectum Pallas fandique secundas
nacta vices, proprie fidens et conscia cause
irriguo sacras haurit de pectore voces: 320

and grew from the foam of the sea and chopped-off testicles. When she might have made Jupiter a father it was really the offspring of you, warlike Mars, and the human race that she was giving birth to! With her this doubtful heir of heaven would have degraded the golden realm with base metal, while he who was unable to earn your fidelity or a night free of worry either with the help of Apollo or with his avenging net, Lemnian Vulcan I mean, he should have gone to avenge the shame of another's disgrace, and forgivingly should not have longed for his own love. And not to mention the Phrygian ..., but who does not know of the most notorious adulteries of this goddess? "But she is gentle, kind and golden." - She gently weaves her deceits, kindly feeds evil and "giltily" seeks reward. There was a time, I remember, when only my power of resisting Jupiter was in evidence. Where was Venus then? Was she the third member in the contest? Where was Pallas? Did she come as the fourth member when summoned? No, indeed, only Juno stood there when Tiresias was judge. But I will say no more. You, Trojan, instead learn to earn the gratitude of Juno who carries the sceptre and bestows gold! The world marvels at such wealth while comets distribute so many kingdoms: choose whatever sceptres and lands you may desire. Whatever you may do, wherever your decision may end, you know that Juno found favour with Jupiter. Judge of Juno, do not despise Jupiter's judgement!' Speaking haughtily in this way she kept firmly in mind her queenly status, adopting a proud look and tone, scorning the mien of a suppliant.

Next into sight comes Pallas who had drawn the right to speak second. Conscious of, and confident in, her own cause, she brings forth these sacred words from her wisdom-giving heart:

Oratio Palladis

'Magna parens superum - nec enim nego, magna Tonantis
nupta, nec invideo - meritum, Frix inclite, nostrum,
si quod erat, carpsit. testor freta, testor Olimpum,
testor humum. non armatas in prelia lingue
credideram venisse deas; hac parte loquacem 325
erubeo sexum, minus hic quam femina possum -
Martem alium didici. victoria feda ubi victus
plus laudis victore feret, nostrisque triumphis
hic haut notus honos. sed quo regina decoro
effatu tendit? dea sit, cedo, immo dearum 330
maxima. non dextre sortiri sceptra potentis
partirive Iovem certatim venimus. illa,
illa habeat que se ostentat. nos gloria saltem
cum titulis opus est ornat minor, et quia cogor
in laudes ire, haut omni sine dote Minerva. 335
si gena, si generis auctor, si denique mores
querendi, in curis regnat pudor, a Iove sanguis,
censori facies oculo patet. heccine forma,
hoc genus, hic mentis cultus? si coniuga dive
gaudia, nuptarum dotes et pignora iactant, 340
virginitas me sola iuvat nil passa pudendum,
non lesura thoros, non deprensura maritos.
macte Paris, mea bella viri, mea pensa puelle
et mea laurigeri meditantur carmina vates.
sic populis utrisque fruor, sic grata per omnes. 345
sed quid ego hec, quid ad hec subnectere plura laborem?
moribus indignum, fateor, studiisque pudicis

Speech of Pallas

The great mother of the gods (a title I do not deny her), who is
also the great bride of Jupiter (and this title I do not envy her)
has impugned whatever merit I had, famous Trojan. I call on the seas,
25 Olympus and the earth to witness this. I had not thought that the
goddesses had come armed for a battle of words; on this point I blush
for the garrulous sex, but I am less capable than a woman here. I
have learned another sort of contest. A victory in which the vanquished
gets more praise than the victor is vile. It is an honour unknown in
30 my victories. But what is our queen driving at with her eloquent speech?
Let her be a goddess - I concede that, even the greatest of the goddesses.
We have not come to compete in casting lots for the sceptres of her
mighty hand or to have a share in Jupiter. Let her keep those things
she has been boasting about. A lesser glory is mine, if praise is
35 essential and since I am forced to sing my own praises, but Minerva is
not totally without assets. If beauty, lineage and morals are in
contention, then modesty rules my emotions, my blood is that of Jupiter
and my beauty is obvious to any judge. Is this not beauty, lineage and
40 refinement? If other goddesses boast of their wedded bliss, their
marriage dowries and their children, I can say that virginity alone
appeals to me. I have not had to put up with anything disgraceful.
I am not going to wreck any marriage or catch any husband doing wrong.
Revered Paris, men think of my battles, girls of my weaving and
45 laurel-crowned poets of my songs. I enjoy the company of both sexes
and am well-received by everyone. But why am I praising myself?
Why am I striving to add even more praise to this? It is degrading
to one's character and to one's modest disposition, I admit,

ostentare suum; proprie nam venditor artis
detitulat titulos, quos ingerit. at quia presens
viribus et viciis armatur causa, Minervam 350
accipe plus tacite meritam quam voce secutam!

Cum vetus efflueret in regnum mobile mundus
terrarumque notas ultrix detergeret unda,
emersit cum sole Fides; mox cetera dudum
nacta fugam virtus terris offensa profanis 355
iam mundo meliore redit: Prudentia numquam
velox, indulgens Pietas, Patientia victrix,
strenua Simplicitas, hilaris Pudor, Ardor Agendi
sobrius et nullo nutans Constantia casu;
non vaga Pax aberat, rerum Concordia custos, 360
Iusticie Rectique Tenor. sine vindice stabant
visure populos et Deucaliona sorores
poscebantque ducem; nec enim secura meandi
copia nec prorsus Furiis in Tartara pulsis
cessavere metus. tandem genitura Minervam 365
contremuit frons celsa Iovis totusque rotatu
intonuit maiore polus, nec letior umquam
lux superis. hoc patre fluens, hoc edita partu
divum pandit iter, Diras et monstra relegat
virtutum custos, virtutum previa Pallas. 370
hec illa est, quam Iuno notat, quam, Dardane, cernis,
marte Minerva potens, hec, cuius dextra minacem
exhausit Flegram. vidi - dicamne? sed omnes
novimus: Encheladi consumpsit flamma Ciclopes,
centimanus pharetras centum Niobesque sagittas 375

to sing one's own praises, for the proclaimer of his own worth
devalues those very claims he advances. But since the present
350 case is being fought on virtues and vices, listen to a Minerva
who has more merit when silent than she will ever have when boasting!

When the old world was washed away into the sea and the avenging
flood cleansed the stains of the earth, Trustworthiness came out with
355 the sun. Immediately the other virtues that had long since fled,
offended by the sinful lands, returned now that the world was
better: Prudence, never in a hurry, kind-hearted Piety,
triumphant Patience, eager Simplicity, cheerful Chastity,
sober Charity and Constancy that does not waver in any
360 misfortune; Peace the traveller's friend, Concord the guardian of
property, and the unswerving course of Justice and Right were also
there. The sisters stood there without a champion, waiting to see
Deucalion and his people, begging for a leader. For there was no
possibility of travelling free from worry, nor had their fears
365 completely disappeared because the Furies had been driven into hell.
At last the lofty brow of Jupiter began to tremble as it gave birth
to Minerva and the whole sky echoed as it turned on a greater axis.
No day was ever more pleasing to the gods. Coming from this father,
370 born in this way, Pallas, the guardian and leader of the virtues,
cleared the path of the gods and banished the Furies and the monsters.
This is the one that Juno criticises, that you see before you, Trojan:
Minerva, powerful in war, whose right hand defeated the threat of
Phlegra. I saw - shall I say it? But we all know the story: how
375 the madness of Enceladus wore out the Cyclopes, the hundred-handed
Briareus scorned the hundred arrows of Diana and Phoebus and the
arrows that killed Niobe,

sprevit, hanelanti iam maior Marte Typhoeus
celum poscebat. ubi tunc Mavortia Iuno?
iuvisset numero saltem propiorque stetisset
pro sceptris armata suis! iam pene supernos
Persephone thalamos Ditem complexa tenebat, 380
cum tandem exiliens trepidis Saturnia stratis
exclamat: "Pallas, Pallas, proh fata, moraris?
pellimur"! accessi. sensit valuisse Medusam
Gorgoneamque deam, sensit, quod fulminat aurum
plus splendore potens, cum celum, sceptra, Penates 385
reddidimus trepide. sit nunc ingrata, sit hostis,
nostrum est, quod regnat, nostrum, quod cum Iove sompno
securo fruitur. at curam imbellis Olimpi
cum subii, tunc diva fui, tunc dicta virago.
vos, superi, testor, quantis sudaverit ausis 390
hoc caput, hoc pectus nostrum,' ac ostendit utrumque
celum suspiciens. 'Pudor hic, hic cassidis horror
et parme, quem Iuno notat. genuitne cerastas
Iupiter? Advertat, cuius convicia tractat,
diva memor parcatque suis! parit illa potentem 395
Vulcanum pariatque velim; non, quod pede molli
militat, invideo, nectitve quod arte catenas'.
sic fatur Veneremque obliquo figit ocello
atque iterat: 'Res o vatum dignissima risu!
en generat voces, evolvit nomina, nugas 400
Pieridum et nostras dignatur noscere frondes.
Sed male vel didicit, meminit vel mollius equo.
vera voce fluit a 'polleo' Pallas et alti
splendorem meriti vix gloria nominis equat.

how Typhoeus got the upper hand as Mars gasped for breath and how he demanded the heavens. And where was warlike Juno then? She could at least have added to the number and approached nearer, armed to

30 defend her rule! Persephone was already on the point of mating with Pluto in the heavenly bed when Saturnian Juno at last jumping out of that bed in fear, shouted: "Pallas, Pallas, by Jupiter! Why are you holding back? We are being driven out!" I moved in. She realised the worth of Medusa the Gorgon goddess then, she realised that the

35 gold of my armour she had criticised was more than just show when I gave her back heaven, her kingdom and her home, as she stood there shaking with fright. She may now be ungrateful and hostile to me, but it is my doing that she is queen, that she can sleep safely with Jupiter. But when I went to the help of feeble Olympus, then I was

90 a 'heavenly one', then I was called a virago. O gods above, I call on you as witnesses to testify to the great deeds of bravery which my head and breast achieved with so much effort.' So saying, she bared both, raising her eyes to heaven. 'Here is the modesty, here the terror of my helmet and shield, reviled by Juno. Did Jupiter

95 produce horned serpents? The goddess should remember and realise whom she is attacking with her insults. She should stop attacking her own! For she produced powerful Vulcan - and I am glad she did; I do not envy her that he goes to war softly or that he is a skilful weaver of nets!' Thus she spoke, and fixing Venus with a sidelong glance, she continued: 'O topic most worthy of the ridicule of poets!

00 She not only etymologises, she gives the derivation of my name, and lowers herself to adopt the trifles of the muses and my leafy crowns. But she has not learned properly, or else her memory is feebler than it should be. In actual fact, Pallas is derived from 'power' and the glory of the name can scarcely compare with the splendour of my lofty merit.

macte Paris - quid enim numerandis improba veris 405
effluo et in titulos suspiro prodiga? - lesi
forte deos, exempla sequor veniamque coactus
error habet. nosti Iunonem indigna locutam,
sed taceo. promsi - fateor doleoque - superba,
vera tamen. sed molle decus formeque triumphum 410
non hac mente peto, viles ut solvar in usus
vulgaresque iocos. hac fronte, hoc oris honore
venatrix hominum vernet Venus! o fuga morum!
diis utinam libranda forem! nunc Cipris in omnes
bella ciet victrixque placet mundumque superbit 415
imperiis cessisse suis. heu, rara securis
aurea, rarus amor morum! quippe ardua frangit
virus dulce, pie Sirtes, amentia supplex,
molle malum, morbus hilaris. sic vendicat orbem
exicium venale Venus, sic exit in omnes 420
teligerum complexa suum exemplumque datura
Vulcano Martique parit. moderantior olim,
mortali contenta iugo non astra coegit
in numerum laqueumque suum, non fulmine blando
fulminis auctorem fregit, non Cinthius ignes 425
maiores miratus erat, non cura Tridentis
in mediis fervebat aquis, sed nomine vero
Bachus Liber erat. pudet, Egeonis alumpna
sera ultrix superos vexat celumque reposcit
cum patrio proiecta gelu cumque exule mentu... - 430
erubeo ulteriora loqui. me strenua certe
omnipotensque Venus temptabat flectere. cessit,
sensi etenim; mecumque utinam deprenderet orbis,

.05 Revered Paris - why do I go on enumerating truths in this shameless fashion and aspire to fame so prodigally? Perhaps I have offended the gods? I am only following Juno's example, and sin that is forced on one is pardonable. You know that Juno said a lot that was unworthy - but I will say no more. I have made, it is true and I regret it, some

.10 proud boasts, but they are truthful. But I do not seek this peaceful honour, this beauty prize, with the intention of earning money from low-class acts of vulgar sex. Venus, the huntress of men, could do really well with this beautiful face of mine! How virtue has fled!

.15 If only I were to be judged by gods! Now the Cyprian wages war against everyone, delights those she defeats, and is proud that the world has yielded to her power. Alas, rare indeed is the golden axe, rare the love of virtue! It is not surprising that this sweet poison, these pious quicksands, this wheedling madness, this soft evil, this happy

.20 disease, weakens firm resolve. Thus Venus, the venal destruction, claims the world, thus she goes out against everyone, embracing her arrow-bearing son. To set an example she has children by both Vulcan and Mars. Once she was less ambitious and was content to yoke mortals: she did not drive gods into her snare to be of her number. She did not

25 destroy the lightning-god with her gentle lightning, Phoebus the Cynthian was not amazed by heat greater than his own. Neptune the trident-god was not steaming with love in the middle of the sea, and Bacchus, true to his name, was free. It is shameful that this child of the sea, this late avenger, harries the gods and claims back the heavens she was

30 thrown out of with her cold father who had lost his pen.. - I blush to say more. The noble, all-powerful Venus certainly tried to influence me, but she failed for I was on my guard. If only the world could deal with her as I did!

quam fallax et blanda venit! nil hoste polito
sevius. omnifico vultu mentita favorem 435
amplexum in planctus solvit, defederat urbes,
arces frangit et in subitum rapit omnia Martem.
cum ventum in cedes, cedit; cum prelia fervent,
frigescit. tunc arma iuvant, tunc Pallas in usu
et Venus in probris. commercia turpia: molles 440
exacuit, duros emasculat et rapit orbem
in predam, cui preda venit. sic mutuus error
invenit alterni solacia digna pudoris.
non cogo in certos numerosum Prothea vultus,
non Venerem semper variam moresque pererro 445
implicitos. satis est, aliquo si cognita nutu
non trahat incautum prorsus. sed voce monentis,
exemplum cui mundus erit, quis dicat egere?
maxime Priamidum, nostra est si gloria quicquid
Mars audet, quod Clio docet, quod tractat Aragne, 450
si tibi mixta manus et partitura Minervam,
si tutoris egent artes et in arce triumphat
Palladium, forme titulum si virgo meretur,
annue et Iliacum, iudex, ne despice fatum'!
desierat vultuque animum vocemque secuto 455
in girum flectens aciem sedet. emicat axe
Ydalio provecta Venus tandemque profatur
mesta parum, sed blanda oculis et fronte serena:

Oratio Veneris

'heu, quibus exilium populis positura relinquar
libera Saturni proles? cui grata vel equa, 460
si superis invisa vagor, si transfuga celi

How deceptively pleasant she is! But there is nothing crueller
35 than a polite enemy. With her changeable face she lies when she
offers you her protection, she turns love into grief. She causes
cities to break treaties, destroys citadels and drives everything
into sudden conflict. When the actual fighting starts she leaves;
in the heat of battle she grows cold. That is when weapons are useful,
that is when Pallas is needed and Venus is reviled. Her changes are
40 disgusting: she makes the weak brave, emasculates the hard men and
makes the world her prey when she comes as prey for it. Thus each
side in error finds some dignified consolation in the shame of the
other. I cannot force versatile Proteus into a recognisable shape
45 and I cannot go over all of Venus' continual changes or her complicated
love intrigues. It is enough if she is recognised by some indication
and does not completely seduce the unwary. But who can say that he
lacks the word of an advisor when the whole world could be an example?
50 O greatest son of Priam, if my glory is whatever Mars dares, what Clio
teaches, what Arachne makes, and if your brothers and sisters need the
different gifts of Minerva, if your skills lack a patron, and if the
Palladium is enthroned in your citadel, or if a virgin deserves the
title of beauty-queen, then give it to her, judge, and do not despise
55 the fate of Troy.' She finished speaking, and with an expression
fitting her thoughts and words she looks around her and sits down.
Venus riding in her Cyprian chariot arrives in haste and speaks at
last somewhat sadly, but her eyes are beautiful and her face calm:

Venus' Speech

60 Alas, I, the free-born daughter of Saturn, to which peoples shall I
be left to take up my exile? To whom shall I be welcome as a friend
if I wander the world, hated by the gods; if, an outcast from heaven

fata sequor? vos, o, spirat quibus orbe secundo
indefessa fides, quos non livescere certum est:
si pia, si facilis, si nulli dura Dione,
pendite, quis causam casus premat, unde tumultus, 465
unde mine! cum prima meos lux extulit ortus,
fovi hominem duros tenere solata labores
et casus miserata graves. sic publica grati
templa michi struxere viri, sic thura merebar.
hinc ire, hinc odii cause. miserescite saltem 470
vos, quibus exul agor! celi rea deprecor orbem,
quem colui; vestram, populi, defendite civem!
flos iuvenum, spes nostra, Paris, non vexo locutas,
non incuso, deas; quis enim vel carpere possit
vel sacros equare modos? at - si qua fatendi 475
libertas veri - nosti, puer inclite, nosti,
que rerum series, steterit quo cardine causa,
quam bene rem sermo digesserit. indice vultu,
eloquio frontis, oculo censore secanda
lis erat. unde igitur armata licentia fandi 480
infremuit? si dura minus reverensque pudoris,
et Iove progenita et virgo Tritonia credi
posset. "at emeruit Musarum maxima dici":
non nego, fingit enim nullique hac arte secunda
falsigraphos commenta docet, docet auribus uti 485
mollibus et cecos per frivola ducere sensus;
cumque per ambages nugis pomposa venustis
Phillidas, Ysiphilas et prelia nostra retractet,
lucratur sacram venalis fabula laurum.
at, si miliciam fingendi feda facultas 490
hanc habitura fuit, saltem discrimen habendum,

I follow my fates? O you whose tireless faith is strong on this good earth, you mortals who certainly feel no jealousy, if I, Dione, am faithful, understanding, cruel to nobody, consider what misfortune assails my case, where the arguments and the threats come from! From the very day of my birth I have cherished man, gently consoling his harsh toil and sympathising with his difficulties and misfortunes. For this reason grateful men have built public temples to me, and I deserved the incense. These are the causes of the anger and hate of the goddesses. You to whom I am driven in exile have pity on me, at least. Accused by the heavens I appeal to the earth that I inhabit: peoples, defend your fellow-citizen. Flower of youth, Paris, my hope, I do not refute or blame the goddesses who have spoken, for who could either fault or emulate their divine manner? But - if I am allowed the possibility of speaking the truth - you know, renowned young man, you know the actual events and on what point this case revolves. You know how well they have explained the problem. This case was to have been judged on the evidence of beauty with our appearance doing the talking and with your eye as the judge. So, how is it that we have had this barbed, aggressive "plain-speaking"? If Tritonian Pallas were less harsh she might be truly thought of as the child of Jupiter. If she were modest she might be convincing as a virgin. "But she is rightly called the greatest of the Muses." That I do not deny, for she is second to none in the art of fiction and teaches fiction-writers their lies. She teaches them to take advantage of gullible audiences and to lead their unwitting senses on to the frivolous. And when our glorious Pallas with her sophisticated speech recalls by allusion the stories of Phyllis and Hypsipyle, and our struggles, her venal poem steals the reward of the sacred laurel from me. But if her vile ability to lie was going to be so aggressive she should at least have been more judicious

in quam, quid, quare! nec enim, si nata cerebro
nostri plena Iovis, gelide nil improba fando
virginis elidit titulum doctissima virgo.
illa virum titulos raptis mendicet ab armis, 495
sit sese contenta Venus. tumide illa minetur,
nos humiles facilesque pati. rorantia tabo
signa ferat victrix, nostri sine cede triumphi.
an, quia nature non obluctata, fatigor?
Anchise si blanda fui, sexumne fefelli? 500
si peperi, cui facta nocens? meus astra Cupido,
Eneas Frigiam vester colit, heccine culpa?
hoc Venus exicium superis molitur et orbi?
hiis homines, hiis dono deos! ergo innuba Pallas
sic merite mores Veneris notet? illane grata, 505
grata viris, quos Marte vorat? placanda puellis,
quarum fastidit sexum? diis digna serenis,
quos resides timidosque vocat? sic exit in omnes,
sic telis placitura suis, sic omnibus equa.
"at virgo est": negat Aglauros, negat anguis opertus. 510
sed taceo. "at facie pollet": consulta reclamat
unda tumorque gene. "gladiis at strenua sumptis":
non proprium, quod fingit, habet. mentita potestas
leta brevi, probrosa diu; post pauca serena
spuria perpetuo sordescit gloria luctu. 515
quondam certa fides bella imperiosa deorum
non una confecta manu, laurusque per omnes
dicta dari. "at victrix Persee Gorgonis umbra
extorsit titulos palmamque imbellis Olimpi":
sic de se meminit Pallas. sic credere oportet, 520

about the who, what and why of the matter! For although she was born fully-grown from the brain of our Jupiter, this most learned virgin destroyed her reputation as a virgin by speaking shamefully. Ler her seek elsewhere the glory of heroes from her violence: let Venus be happy with what is more fitting for her. Let her be arrogant and threatening: I am humble and long-suffering. Let her carry her standards dripping with gore: my triumphs are bloodless. Or am I assailed because I did not fight my nature? If I was intimate with Anchises did I betray my sex? If I gave birth to Aeneas, whom did I harm? My son Cupid lives in heaven, your Aeneas lives in Phrygia: is this a sin? Is this Venus' way of plotting ruin for heaven and earth? With these I endow men and gods! So unmarried Pallas would criticise the morals of Venus who is thus meritorious? Is she popular - popular, I mean, with men she destroys in war? Is she to be revered by girls whose sex she rejects? Does she deserve to be among the serene gods she calls sluggish and cowardly? This is the way she attacks everyone, going to please them with her weapons, friendly to one and all. "But she is a virgin." Aglauros would not agree, nor the serpent that was shut away. But enough of that. "But she has a beautiful face." The reflection of her swollen cheeks in the water cries out against this. "But she is a good fighter." What is assumed is not one's own. Power that is not true brings a short period of happiness and a long period of disgrace; after a short honeymoon borrowed glory becomes base with permanent grief. There was a time when it was known for certain that the power-struggle of the gods was not decided by one single person and that the laurels were awarded to all of them. "But the conquering shade of the Gorgon of Perseus has snatched the glory and the honour of cowardly Olympus." That is what Pallas says about herself, so you ought to believe it.

crede, Paris! res digna fide tradendaque fastis:
plus Iove, plus Phebo, potuit plus femina Marte,
Marte utinamque meo! nec enim tibi, Iuno, nepotes
invideo - si digna tamen - nec turpe Minervam
ut socium numerare genus. tot freta Dione 525
vindicibus potuit, saltem si fata tulissent,
serpentum non esse parens miserique per urbem
exulis explicito raperet vestigia giro
Hermione Martis. vidi, vidi ipsa nefande
cesum, quem peperit, populum'. sic fata madentem 530
inclinat vultum rursusque accensa profatur:
'de fatis nil lesa queror, metuenda deorum
invidia est. blando Semele conceperat astro,
plena deo, paritura deum, denusque tumebat
mensis, cum vultum Iuno mentita severum 535
accedit, persuadet, abit. quid credula, simplex,
inscia iurato premitur Iove? sic tua longis,
Cadme, fides perspecta viis, sic annuus error
emeruit? cum rapta soror viduamque parares
Iunonem sancire Iovi, te luctibus ecce 540
munerat inque tuos flammis armatur alumpnos.
gaudeat, en quali deitas rugosa triumpho
molitur titulos! tremula dum militat hasta,
altricis mentita fidem. nam cetera nullus
confinxisse labor; faciles ad tempora cani, 545
ad faciem veniunt ruge; fallenda senectus,
non fingenda fuit. o si ad certamina forme
illa potens Beroe staret socianda Dione
incuteret celebrem simulatrix simia risum!

Go on, Paris - believe it! It is a story that deserves to be believed, fit to be put in the history books: a woman achieved more than Jupiter, Phoebus Apollo and my Mars - ah, if only he were mine! But Juno, I do not begrudge you your grandchildren - if I am not too presumptuous, that is - nor am I ashamed to count Minerva as a relative. Relying on so many defenders, I, Venus, should have been able not to become the mother of snakes, and Hermione, my daughter by Mars, would not be crawling along through the city of a miserable exile - at least if the Fates had been willing! I myself witnessed the impious slaughter of the many children she produced.' Thus speaking, she lowers her tear-stained eyes, but then continues again, angrily: 'I do not complain of being harmed by the Fates: it is the jealousy of the gods that has to be feared. Semele had conceived under a favourable star, and pregnant by a god she was going to give birth to a god. She was in the tenth month of her pregnancy when Juno, disguised as an old woman, arrives, persuades and leaves. Why is credulous, simple, naive Semele destroyed by the oath of Jupiter? Cadmus, is this what your faith earned you on that year-long journey? When your sister, Europa, was abducted, and you were working to reconcile abandoned Juno with Jupiter, Juno rewards you with grief and attacks your children with lightning. Let her be happy, for you can see with what a triumph the wrinkled deity earns her glory! While her weapon is a trembling walking-stick she only has to adopt the faithful character of a nurse. It was no great task to have feigned the rest; white hair comes easily to her temples, wrinkles to her face. In fact, she had to hide her senility, not feign it. O if only that powerful Beroe were standing here now to be judged alongside Dione in the beauty contest her ape-like appearance would cause hoots of laughter!

stulte, quid Europen genero Iove queris, Agenor? 550
illa rapi meruit, raptorem excusat egestas
et thalami pocioris amor. sibi maxima debet
quod tociens vidua est coniunx Iovis. alite fausto
nupsisset stabilique thoro, si prima tulissent
federa plus forme, lingue minus. improba, turpis, 555
garrula legitimi mores incestat amantis.
"at soror est coniunxque Iovis": bene cessit in uno,
coniugis offensam redimit soror. "ardua regnat":
at patris in solio fruiturque iugalibus astris
stirpis non thalami merito. fuit aureus olim 560
ille senex, quo nata feror, fuit unicus heres,
necdum sortilegam mundus nutabat in urnam,
cum pia Saturni proles, equanda Minerve
vel saltem non exul erat. regnoque tirannis
concedente tribus triplicem processit in orbem 565
communis regina Venus; quod cum Iove Iuno,
cum Iove cum Tritone fuit cum Dite Dione;
non mea sideribus famulis contenta potestas,
tartara solatur, mulcet freta. vos, pia ponti
turba, dee vestre scelus excusate sororis, 570
si scelus hinc traxisse genus; tuque, optima vindex,
imperiosa Thetis, celum Iunone fugata
posce tuum raptasque faces! iam pelice pulsa,
iam non sollicito venies paritura Tonanti,
fatis nulla fides. precium Saturnia forme 575
perdet, opes perdet. non huc emptura decorem
venisset, si pulcra domi. male, Dardane, mores
consuluit dare promta tuos. non flectitur auro,

50 Agenor, you fool, why do you want Europa back from your son-in-law Jupiter? She deserved to be abducted. His lack of a beautiful wife plus the desire for a better sex-life both excuse Jupiter's abduction of her. Jupiter's wife has only herself to blame if she is deserted so often. She would have married under a favourable auspice, enjoying a stable relationship, if the marriage-contract had

55 contained more beauty and less talk. A shameless, despicable, garrulous wife causes her husband to commit adultery. "But she is the wife and sister of Jupiter." That has turned out well in one respect - the fact that she is his sister makes up for the offence she gives as his wife. "She rules on high." On her father's throne, and she enjoys her conjugal

60 heaven because of her birth not because of her marriage. Once there was a golden old man whose daughter I am said to be. He was the unique inheritor of the universe. As yet the universe had not been put into the fortune-teller's urn, and the pious daughter of Saturn was the equal of

65 Minerva, or at least was not an exile. When the universe was divided among the three tyrants Venus went into all three parts as the joint queen. What Juno shares with Jupiter I, Dione, shared with Jupiter, Neptune and Pluto. My power is not content with the heavens as servants, it brings consolation in hell and calm to the seas. You pious female

70 deities of the sea, forgive the crime of your sister goddess, if crime it be to have one's origins in the sea; and you, great avenger, imperious Thetis, cast out Juno and demand the heaven that is yours with your aborted marriage! Once the whore has been driven out you will come to bear children to the Thunderer, who will not be afraid. There is no

75 trust to be had in the Fates. Saturnian Juno will squander the beauty-prize and riches. She would not have come here to buy beauty if she was beautiful at home already. Trojan, she who is ready to bribe you did not think very carefully about your character. He is not impressed by gold

qui titulum paritatis habet. victricibus olim
armentis impensa fides librantis habene 580
non vendit nutum, veteris non immemor equi.
illane, blande Paris, vultu victore fruetur,
cui gemit Hesione, sanguis cui fluxit avitus,
Alcide que tela sui libravit in arces,
bellica virgo, tuas? ubi tunc que prelia iactas, 585
fatum ubi? plus actum est rapto Frige; pocula nate
eripuit thalamumque dee sic molliter ultus
aspera, miscet adhuc superis dotatus Olimpo.

Flos Asie, veneranda deum regumque propago
non meus instabiles labor est aut gloria versus 590
texere, non trepidas pensis urgere puellas,
nec mecum Phebus, mecum certavit Aragne;
hos Pallas tibi pacta pedes, hec stamina nectat.
plurima dii - fateor - faciles et summa pacisci
et dare; sed quid opes, quid regna, quid arma potenti 595
adiciunt, cuius sceptrum pars amplior orbis,
cuius opes Frigie, cuius gens Dardana vires?
at si solanda est thalami regalis egestas,
si vires, si sceptra nichil sine coniugis usu,
munus habe Veneris, munus quo Sparta superbit, 600
munus quod Iuno dici velit, esse Minerva!
quid moror? internam propius rimare Dionem,
res agitur tractanda palam, iam pectora nuda
pandimus: hac facie Phebo duce metior astra,
hoc vultu produco diem. formose, merenti 605
gratare et similem, iudex, ne despice vultum!'
sic effata genas rapto depromit amictu

who has the reputation for impartiality. That fairness once applied
80 to the winning bulls does not money the verdict of the poised scales,
forgetting its sense of justice. Charming Paris, will she win the
beauty-contest, she who caused Hesione to lament and made your
grandfather's blood flow? She who aimed the spears of her protege
Hercules at your citadels, warlike Pallas? Where was your boasted
85 battle prowess then? Where was Fate? More was achieved by an
abducted Trojan: he snatched the marriage bed from the goddess Juno
and the goblets from her daughter, thus avenging peacefully the harsh
deeds of Juno. He still mixes drinks for the gods, well provided
for on Olympus.

Flower of Asia, honourable offspring of gods and kings, it is not my
90 task or glory to weave unstable verses or to impose my spindles on
frightened girls. Phoebus did not compete against me, nor did Arachne;
Pallas promised you the verses, let her weave your wool. The gods are
quick to agree several good contracts and to honour them, I admit, but
95 what can riches, dominions or arms bring to a powerful man whose
kingdom is greater than half the world, whose riches are Phrygia, and
whose strength is the Trojan people? But if the lack of a royal marriage
bed is to be remedied, if power and dominion are nothing without the
00 presence of a wife, then take the gift of Venus, a gift that Sparta is
proud of, a gift that Juno would like to be called and Minerva actually
to be! But why do I waste my time? Find out about the inner Venus at
close hand. This business needs to be seen in the open. Look at my
05 naked breasts: with this beauty I follow the sun around the heavens,
with this charm I start off the day. Handsome judge, reward a deserving
candidate, and do not reject a face as beautiful as yours!' So saying,
she tears off her cloak and reveals her face.

nuda humeros, exerta sinus totoque diescit
ore. pudet divas Veneri cessisse triumphum.

'consulite, ultores Frigii, Venus excitat egros. 610
hac constant michi visa fide, vel sompnia certe
pondus habent. hec fata sequor. parete Dione,
que civi lacrimas, risus que terminet hosti!'

Her body was naked, her bared breasts glistened in total beauty. The other goddesses were ashamed that they had yielded the victory to Venus.

510 Take note you Trojan avengers: Venus stirs up the down-hearted. What I have seen corresponds to this belief and dreams really do have substance. These are the Fates I follow. Obey Dione who will put an end to the grief of Troy and the laughter of the Greek enemy.

Liber tercius de raptu Helene

Solvuntur vario consulta silentia plausu.
Ydalium Peana canunt plebs, aula, senatus.
hic fatis vovet, ille deis, una omnibus una
voce animoque frequens plaudit Venus. altus ubique
sanguis obit, sacris ultro cessantia cedunt 5
arva, coronato luget spoliata marito
Inachis et raptos gemebunda reposcit alumpnos.
illustres superis epulas molita potestas
sacrificis bibulos lictoribus instruit ignes
totaque thuricremis Panchaia spirat in aris 10
venales emptura deos. at pauper acerra
principe digna Deo nostro placitura Tonanti
mente litat pura, votis exorat honestis.
celsior explicitas rapturus in ardua flammas
regius exstruitur congestis floribus ignis 15
perstringitque aciem. procul hiis exspirat ab aris
hostia dira, cruor; Veneri quod dulce propinat
ductor, Aristeos latices, Melibea fluenta,
Ycareos haustus, fracti Phenicis odores.
fronde comas nexe sanctoque astare parenti 20
Yliades iusse spumantia lacte serenis

Third Book - The Abduction of Helen

The silence of the deliberations is broken by much applause. The ordinary people, the court and the elders sing the praises of Venus. One prays to the Fates, another to the gods, and the name of Venus alone is joyfully lauded again and again in every heart and mouth. Everywhere the blood of fat sacrificial animals runs as the fields, doomed to inactivity, gladly yield up their bulls for sacrifice. The heifer lows in grief for the loss of her garlanded mate and sighs for the return of her calves that are led off to their ritual slaughter. The most important townspeople strive to prepare a splendid banquet for the gods while tending the thirsty flames for the sacrificing priests. The whole of Arabia goes up in smoke on the incense-burning altars to bribe the venal gods. However, the poor man's incense-box is worthy of the greatest God and will be acceptable to our Thunderer because he entreats with honourable vows. A pure mind is the sacrifice for Him. Priam's altar fire, piled high with masses of aromatic herbs, dazzles the eyes. It is bigger than the others in order to send its flames unhindered to the heavens. Far away from these altars the blood gushes out from a grim sacrifice. For Venus the king offers what is sweet - honey, milk, wine and perfumes. With flowers in their hair the daughters of Priam assist their holy father as directed,

cimbia devolvunt flammis, rex ipse ministrans
Ydaliam delibat avem sic ante precatus:

Supplicatio Priami ad Venerem

'Diva potens hominum, divum imperiosa voluptas,
vera deum soboles, nostri Tritonis alumpna, 25
alma Venus! seu te convivam Thetios urna
poscit seu nectar superum seu forte papaver
Elisium, flecte hec teneros ad dona iugales,
hos dignare favos! nec enim mactante securi
grata minus pia sacra tibi. si digna litamus, 30
exorata veni pariterque haustura recumbe!
celsa licet caleant centeno thure Cithera,
Ydalium modulos nectat nemus, ardua Cypri
in flores crescant varios: incensa Cithera,
Ydalias volucres, Cypri thima Pergama vincent. 35
hiis meritis, hiis, si qua tamen, veneranda Dione,
adde fidem visis, sponsi memor adde favorem,
solatam solare domum! non improbus oro
ut tuus Inachias iudex predetur alumpnas;
Hesione contentus eat. Tritonia certe 40
non neget hosque velit melior Saturnia raptus.
olim Asie - sed quid vulgata ac flenda revolvo? -
claruit imperium, formidandusque Pelasgis
Frix erat; inversa est vetus alea. respice, diva,
Eneadas miserare tuos!' sic fatus in ignes 45
Ybleas inclinat opes, ieiunaque spirans
nidor odorifero solatur sidera fumo.

pouring cups of foaming milk on the bright flames, while the king himself sacrifices, touching the Idalian bird after praying thus:

Priam's Prayer to Venus

'O powerful goddess of men, imperious delight of the deities, true offspring of the gods, child of our Tritonian Neptune, beloved Venus! Whether an urn of seawater can bring about your presence, or the nectar of the gods, or perhaps the Elysian poppy, turn your gentle pair of doves towards these gifts and deign to accept these honeycombs! For these pious offerings are no less welcome to you than a sacrifice from an axe. If our sacrifices are worthy, come when you are entreated. Sit down with us and drink! Although Mount Cythera may burn with a hundred altars, the forest of Idalium may have the billing and cooing of its doves, and the heights of Cyprus their brightly-coloured flowers, nevertheless Pergamum will surpass the incense of Cythera, the Idalian birds and the aromatic herbs of Cyprus. Confirm these merits, reverend Venus; confirm this dream if it is to be believed. Remember the husband-to-be and grant your approval. Console a devastated family! I do not pray wickedly that your judge should abduct Greek women; let him leave Greece satisfied to have Hesione. Tritonian Pallas will certainly not show any opposition and indeed Saturnian Juno will even welcome the abduction. Once, - but why do I repeat things that are common knowledge and painful? - once the power of Asia was famous and the Phrygians struck fear into the Greeks. But the old order has been overturned. Look upon us, goddess, and have pity on the people of your son, Aeneas!'

Having prayed thus, he pours the Hyblaean honey into the flames, and the rising scent of the aromatic smoke satisfies the hungry heavens.

Vaticinium Heleni

Iam votis sacrisque modus, iam fessa reclinat
flamma apices, alios Helenus prorumpit in estus
bachantemque deum flagranti pectore nactus 50
vocales tripodum Furias angustat in usus
orsus ita: 'heu Frigii, gens non premensa futurum!
quo noster spoliator abit? quenam illa carina,
que Troiam mersura redit, iam litora tangit?
ite duces contra!' sic interrupta profatus 55
plus dubios urit, pleno tamen arguit ore
Deiphebum, cui summa fides et sola medendi
copia, iussa sequi Veneris, raptum ire Lacenas,
auctores sperare deos. 'quenam ista nefanda
spes?', inquit. 'superumne fides celique potestas 60
incestum dispenset iter, predantibus assit?
macte Paris, sceleris alios molire ministros
et sompnum tibi finge novum! non fallere norunt,
qui falli nequeunt.' orantem haut sustinet ultra
Troilus, utque animo preceps bellique sititor 65
et gladii consultor erat, 'timidissime fratrum,
vade' ait, 'o tenebris antri dampnate loquacis,
vade, inquam, et quociens visum tibi fallere plebem,
finge deum! nobis alius iam constat Apollo.
ibit Alexander. non, si Cumana senectus 70
aut aries Libicus aut Chaonis obstrepat ales,
iussum flectet iter. ibit miseramque reducet,
quod nolles, tamen Hesionen.' conclamat herilem
preceps ad nutum plebes; excire tumultus,
quos nequeat sopire, potens nec mensa futurum 75

The Prophecy of Helenus

And now with an end to the prayers and the sacrifices, when the flames began to weaken and falter, Helenus breaks out in another sort of heat. Receiving the raging god in his burning breast he struggles to give voice to the frenzied stimulus from the tripod, saying: 'Alas, Phrygians, race that has no thought for the future! Where is our pirate going? What is this ship now reaching the shore, only to return to destroy Troy? Oppose this, leaders!' Speaking in bursts like this he puts the doubting Trojans in greater torment, and then openly accuses Deiphobus, who alone was to be fully trusted and who alone could remedy their grief, of following Venus' orders, of going to abduct Spartan women, and of believing that the gods sanctioned this. What is this wicked hope?' he asks. 'Does the good faith of the gods or the might of heaven assign this evil journey to you? Or give help to plunderers? Revered Paris, invent other instigators for your crime. Dream something different. The gods who cannot be deceived do not know how to deceive.' Troilus cannot tolerate him speaking any longer, headstrong, warmonger and sword-happy as he is. 'O most cowardly of brothers', he says, 'go on. Go on, I say, cursed by the darkness of the jabbering grotto, and each time you wish to mislead the people pretend it is a god. The Apollo we know is different. Paris will go. If the old Sybil of Cumae or the ram of Libya or the birds of Chaonia should loudly clamour against it, he will not alter the itinerary that has been commanded. He will go, and moreover will bring back poor Hesione against your will.' The people applaud, always ready to follow a leader's whim: capable of stirring up trouble they cannot settle. Not having weighed up the consequences they are bold since for the moment they feel no fear.

audet, cum presens metuat nichil. omnibus arma,
arma animis mentique frequens illabitur Argo
Laomedonque iacens et inulte dedecus urbis,
conclamantque iterum: 'quonam usque, o libera pubes
Dardanio cognata Iovi, patiemur inultum 80
tot iugulos rubuisse senum, tot colla parentum
Argea nutasse manu? non impia sanxit
Atropos hoc etiam nostris incumbere fatis,
ultorem non posse dari. si numinis iram
Troia merens sensit, penas quoque iudice Phebo 85
dira Micenee debent convivia mense.
ite, duces, Venus hec, hec certior augur Apollo
bella iubet fratrumque exhausta funditus urbe
poscit inoffensos Frigio ductore meatus.
unde metus, metus unde, viri? concessit in ignes 90
indutus Nessum Tirynthius, ecce timoris
causa prior cessit. spirat par Herculis Hector,
ecce animos gens nostra dabit. si prima Pelasgis
laurea, fas Frigibus palmam sperare secundam
et nostros rediisse deos. vos, inclita saltem 95
pignora, cesorum iugulos lugete parentum!
vos, quibus uberior lacrimas iniuria nectit,
vos pietas armata vocat.'

Vaticinium Panthi

sic voce precantur
intenduntque manus, egras cum Panthus in aures
fatorum monitus priscos serit et, quod ab ipsis 100
extorsit genitor aditis Euforbius, index

The desire for arms and yet more arms comes to everybody's heart,
and the thought of the Argo comes frequently to mind as does that of
the prostrate Laomedon and the disgrace of their unavenged city.
They burst into voice again: 'Just how long, o free race, kin of
Jupiter through Dardanus, shall we allow to go unavenged the fact
that so many of our elders' throats were stained with blood, or
that the heads of our parents tottered because of a Greek hand?
Pitiless Atropos did not sanction that this too, should
form part of our fates, that is the denial of an avenger.
If Troy deservedly felt the god's anger, then the grim feasts
of the Mycenean table deserve to suffer too, from Apollo's
judgement. Go forth, leaders. Both Venus and Apollo,
a more reliable augur, order this war and demand a safe return for
the Phrygian leader after the total destruction of the city of the
brothers. Where is the cause for your fears, men? The Tirynthian hero
has put on the shirt of Nessus and burned to death, so the foremost
cause for fear has gone. Hector flourishes, the equal of Hercules,
so that our very nationality will give us courage. If the first
victory fell to the Greeks it is only right for Trojans to expect
that our gods have returned to us to give us the second. You, glorious
offspring, at least mourn the slit throats of your slaughtered parents!
You, whose greater loss brings you tears, armed piety summons you.'

The Prophecy of Panthus

Such are the prayers they voice when they stretch out their hands,
and then Panthus plants in their sick ears the original warnings
of the Fates; what his father, Euphorbius, had wrested from the
very shrines of the gods

in medium pandit proles: 'lapsura sub Argis
Pergama, si Frigias Helene conscendat in urbes'.
hiis iam facta fides ducibus vulgique tumultus
flectitur. o quanto priscis nova mollius urgent! 105
plus superi constant Pantho memorante futura
quam dicente Heleno. Priami tamen egra lacessit
consilia Hesione; superos premit, audit et audet
dux falli fatisque favet, cum fata recuset,
atque ita: 'dic' inquit, 'alio dic ordine fata, 110
Anthenor, memora iam facta! necesse peractum
constat, venturum mutabile transit. habemus
iam cunctis graviora minis: perfusa cruore
Pergama, nuptarum lacrimas, lamenta parentum.
tu quoque visa refer, Frigie repetitor alumpne, 115
atque ea que passus obiter tot cladibus adde!
hiis saltem cedat bachantis fabula fani
et moneat potiora fides. prius esse negabit
unda fluens, ignis urens, spirabilis aer,
quam dictet facienda furor.' sic fatur, at ille 120
'ergo' ait, 'o cives, iterum testanda laborum
historia. an lapsa est necdum vetus? indice questu
non opus est, ubi regna dolos et bella loquuntur.
vidimus emeritis fecundam civibus urbem
atque alium regnare ducem. nondum Ylios Argis 125
cesserat. hasne vices velox oblivio transit
inmemor et longi precidit tedia luctus
inpaciens languere diu? quin, inclita pubes,
si iuvat inviso mentes absolvere questu,
armata decurre manu! fortuna sequenda est, 130

he, the son, reveals to all: 'Troy will fall to the Greeks if Helen enters the Phrygian cities'. So the established trust in the future of the leaders and the clamour of the people are changed. O how the new has less impact than the old! The gods are more in evidence in what Panthus recalls of the future than in what Helenus says. However, the thought of Hesione troubles the wavering Priam. The king crushes the gods' replies; he hears them but dares to be deceived, and so defers to destiny though he rejects their evidence. So he says: 'Tell us, Antenor, tell us the future in another way. Recall what has already happened! It is necessarily true that the past is fixed but that the future is subject to change. We now have something worse than all the warning signs: Pergamum is drenched with blood, brides are in tears, parents are lamenting. Tell us too, what you saw, you the seeker of the Trojan girl, and add to so many disasters the account of those things you suffered en route! Let the lie of the mad shrine make way for these words, at least, and let what is reliable urge a better course. Water will refuse to be liquid, fire to be igneous and air to be breatheable before madness will dictate what must be done.' Thus he speaks, and then Antenor says: 'So, citizens, the story of my tribulations must be told again. Is the story, which is not yet ancient, forgotten already? There is no need for my lament to bear witness when our kingdom testifies to treachery and war. We have seen a rich city inhabited by worthy citizens, another king on the throne. Troy had not yet yielded to the Greeks. Has swift, forgetful oblivion traversed these misfortunes and cut short the boredom of a long grief because it cannot bear to mourn for long? Why, glorious youth, if it is any pleasure to rid your minds of hated grief, then attack with weapons in your hands! Fortune has to follow

dum preclarum aliquid dolor indecoctus hanelat.
nil grande et longum; segnem timor obruit iram.
heretis quia fana vetant? hec scilicet angit
cura deos evi tacitos vexare recessus
et rerum librare vices. stant fixa tenore 135
fata suo. certam miseris si Parca ruinam
indixit Frigibus, moriendum Marte; triumphum
si pepigit, meritum minuit victoria segnis.
o falli faciles! si fas depromere verum,
deprendi insidias superum. Lerneus Apollo 140
nostras vexat aves et que metuenda minatur
Dardanidis timet ipse suis. sic ficta locutus
accinctos ad bella Friges prevertere temptat.
vos contra cunctis potiora eventa futuris
pendite: donatos Tirynthius induit ignes, 145
Eacide senuere duo nullique timendus
aut puer aut virgo est, quem fata minantur, Achilles.
ipse, viri, vidi ipse viros et menia, vidi
urbes, sed gelidos nil excitat. ite, potentes,
et iugulos aptate iugo spretoque triumpho 150
reddite fatidicis victores hostibus enses!'
hiis virtus accensa viris, procul omnis abacta
relligio. cedit Helenus vittasque minaces
abicit et lacrimis incusat fata secutis.

Profectio Paridis ad rapiendam Helenam

Dux cepti legitur pastor Paris, advena quondam 155
regni, nunc regis heres; nec profuit urbi
fatalem dampnasse facem, cum lederet ardens

when still-fermenting grief craves for something glorious.
Nothing great is long drawn out. Fear destroys anger that is
sluggish. Do you hesitate because the shrines forbid? Indeed, this
pursuit forces the gods to trouble the silent recesses of future time
35 and to consider the destiny of things. Destiny stands fixed in its
course. If the Fates have decided on certain ruin for the wretched
Trojans we ought to die in war. If they have promised triumph then
a half-hearted victory diminishes the merit. O easily deceived men!
40 If it is right to utter the truth I have uncovered the deceit of the
gods. Apollo of Lerna is troubling our birds of augury, and the fears
he threatens the Trojans with he actually feels for his own Greeks.
By speaking such lies he attempts to divert the Trojans already armed
for battle. On the other hand consider the actions that are more
45 cogent than all prognostications of the future: Hercules has put on
the shirt of fire he was given, the two sons of Aeacus have grown old,
while Achilles, whom the fates threaten us with either as a boy or a
girl, is to be feared by nobody. Men, I have seen for myself their
warriors and their fortifications. I have seen their cities. Nothing
50 rouses the cowardly. Go on, you mighty fighters, fit your necks to the
yoke, and spurning a triumph as victors, hand back your swords to your
prophetic opponents!' At these words courage is kindled in the men;
all sense of religion is banished far off. Helenus leaves, throwing
away his fillets of foreboding. In tears he reproaches the Fates.

The Journey of Paris to abduct Helen

55 As leader of the expedition is chosen the shepherd, Paris. Once a stranger
to the kingdom he is now the king's heir. It was no use to that city that
it had condemned the lethal torch when the burning

pregnantem sompnus Cisseida; pullulat alte
flamma vetus revehuntque fidem presagia plenam.
it fati imperio Danaum rapturus alumpnam 160
Dardanus et blande debellaturus Achivos
prevelat fraudes. cesas non induit alnos
pinnarum suspecta strues, numerosa vagatur
tranquillo classis cultu; regalis olivam
pretendit pinus tandemque erepta furori 165
semimaris Galli non adversante Cibebe
miratur similes bachari ad litora voces.
hanc decor insignit, qualem progressior usus
post longum lucratur opus: tabulata superbis
preradiant inscripta notis, vestitur herili 170
prora Tiro puppisque Tago, nitor erigit Indus
antempnam spargitque in transtra cupressus odorem
vela regens. certant venti, quis linthea tendat
purpureos discincta sinus, at lene fluentes
arcessit Zephiros puppi prescripta Dione. 175
instabat iam dicta dies, qua classis in altas
propulsum poscebat aquas, cum lecta iuventus
Priamiden sortita ducem per litora ferri
discursu rapido, qualisque abeuntibus ardor,
certatim fremere et varios miscere tumultus. 180
haut mora, succincto Nabatheos agmine ducens
Hector in arma Friges comites per cerula fratri
ire iubet, certantque rates stipare secuti
Peonide duce Deiphebo, quin ipse Diones
spes Anchisiades cum Polidamante secundo 185
iungit opes. iamque effractas rapiebat harenas

dream afflicted the pregnant Hecuba: the flame of long ago grows
big and the omens are coming to full fruition. At the command of
160 Fate the Trojan Paris sets sail to abduct the Greek girl. Going
to defeat the Greeks by charm he veils his treachery. No suspicious
cluster of pinnacles clothes his hollow ships. His large fleet sails
165 under peaceful guise. An olive-branch decks his royal ship which
started life as a pine tree violently uprooted to the frenzy of an
effeminate Gallus with Cybele's approbation. It marvels that similar
voices howl at the shore. A decoration such as a more advanced
technique achieves after long toil distinguishes this ship: the boards
170 shine with their covering of superb paintings, the prow is clothed
with royal purple and the stern with gold. The sailyard is of ivory
while the cypress mast spreads its perfume along the thwarts as it
governs the sails. The winds compete to see which can stretch the
175 billowing sails into purple breasts, but an image of Venus attracts
the gently blowing zephyrs to the ship. The appointed day was now
dawning when the fleet longed to be launched on to the deep sea and
then the selected band of youths under their chosen leader, Paris,
180 rush across the beach - such is the enthusiasm of the voyagers -
shouting to each other and raising a confused uproar. There is no
delay. Leading the Nabathaeans in battle dress Hector orders them
to go as armed Phrygian companions for his brother across the seas.
Under the leadership of Deiphobus the Paeonians follow and hurry
185 to pack into their ships. Even Aeneas, son of Anchises and hope
of Venus, with Polydamas as his lieutenant, adds his support.
Already the fleet was dragging the scattered sand

in pelagus classis humerosque manusque secuta,
cum tandem exclamans aditis Cassandra relictis
fata aperit turbatque Friges. at seva morantes
impellit Lachesis pinus uncosque tenaces 190
rumpit et intento percellit flamine vela.
ultimus in socias fatalis predo carinas
provehitur multum Priamo frustraque rogatus,
ne quicquam temere victori supplicet hosti,
Hesione contentus eat; sin reddere raptam 195
velle negent, bellum intentet. sic format iturum
venturosque Friges accepto interprete spondet.

Vix in conspectum Paridi patuere Cithera,
cum patrias permensus aquas ad Nestora casu
Atrides molitus iter, Simoontide pinu 200
perspecta secum volvit, qui, quo, unde; stupentque
alternis reges figentes lumina velis.
en, qua fata fide rerum discrimina nectant:
hostis adest, Menelaus abest geminosque Lacones
Hermione sibi nacta duces Agamennonis urbem 205
visum ierat matrem cupide visura secundam;
plebs quoque Iunoni celebrem confluxerat Argos
ludificum ductura diem, pontusque vacabat
et tellus exuta viris. sic omnia casus
expediit ventura potens victrixque Dione. 210

Prodit in abruptum pretentis insula saxis
mirtigere sacrata dee, pars ima recessu
abditiore iacens refugos falcatur in arcus
depressos furata sinus. huc litore blando

into the sea and moving under the impetus of shoulders and arms, when at the last moment Cassandra leaves the god's shrine, shouting as she reveals the fates and troubling the Trojans. But cruel Lachesis drives on the lingering ships, breaks free the restraining anchors and strikes the sails with a fierce blast of wind. Paris, the death-bringing pirate, is the last to join his companion ships, having been earnestedly entreated in vain by Priam not to ask the victorious enemy rashly for anything but to leave content with Hesione. But if they refuse the return the captive then he should threaten them with war. Thus he instructed Paris on the point of departure, promising that the Phrygians would come if he, Paris, sent a messenger for assistance.

Scarcely had the island of Cerigo come into Paris' sight when Menelaus, son of Atreus, who happened to be crossing his territorial waters en route for a visit to Nestor, catches sight of the Trojan fleet and wonders who they are, where they are going and where they have come from. The princes are amazed as they fix their eyes on each other's sails. See how steadfastly the Fates weave the dangers for the world: the enemy is at hand, Menelaus leaves while Hermione under the protection of Castor and Pollux had gone to visit Agamemnon's city eagerly in order to see her maternal aunt. The people too had converged on famed Argos to celebrate Juno's festal day. The sea was deserted and the countryside bereft of men. Thus Fate which has power and victorious Venus prepared for all that was to come.

The island sacred to the myrtle-bearing goddess rises steeply with its rocky cliffs. The farthest part, lying in a deep recess, is scythed out in receding curves, taking the form of gentle harbours. Trusting in the safe beach

freta Frigum pubes puppes agit. ipse propinquas 215
sanguine sacrifico Latoidos irrigat aras
princeps et larga cumulat promissa securi.
ergo Citheriacas preceps it fama per urbes
Priamiden venisse Parim, plebs undique portus
occursu complet. at pollens ore Lacena 220
ignotos visura viros ad litora gressus
dirigit acclinemque freto defertur Heleam.

Postquam Helenes Paridi patuit presentia, classem
deserit ac forme fidens et conscius oris
huc illuc gressum librans, qua Tindaris ibat, 225
indefessa vagis incessibus ocia texit
certantesque offert vultus, incendia nutrit
mutua captatumque brevi lucratur amorem.
quippe nec ad cursum preceps nec segnior equo
librato gestu formam iuvat, auctus in armos, 230
in caput erectus. tenero delibat harenam
incessu figitque oculo mirante Lacenam
oblitosque gradus sistit; suspectus haberi
mox metuens transfert celeres ad cetera visus,
ceu stupeat quicquid spectat. moderantius illa 235
obliquos vultus et non ridentia plene
ora gerit totasque velit cum pectore nudo
ostentare genas, sed castigator adultos
comprimit excessus animi pudor, egraque mixtus
pulsat corda metus. sentit Paris, ardet et audet, 240
promissorque ingens facilis presagia prede
ducit amor. dum signa iuvant, dum nutus oberrat,

the Trojan youths land their ships here. The leader, Paris, sprinkles the nearby altars of Diana with sacrificial blood and piles up offerings killed by the broad axe. And so Rumour spreads rapidly through the cities of the island that Paris, son of Priam, had come. From all around citizens congregate to fill the harbour to see him. But Helen of the beautiful face directs her steps to the shore to see these unknown men and is brought to Helea, a city overlooking the sea.

When the presence of Helen becomes known to Paris he leaves the fleet, trusting in his beauty and aware of his handsome features. Going wherever Helen goes he spends his time tirelessly walking up and down, inciting her to look at him and feeding their mutual passions. In a short time he captures and wins her love. Indeed, neither walking too quickly nor more slowly than normal, he enhances his beauty by his poise and balance, with his broad shoulders and head held high. He walks lightly across the beach, eyeing Helen with an approving look, then stops, forgetting to continue his stride. Then, fearing to be thought acting suspiciously, he quickly transfers his gaze to other things as if amazed at all he sees. Showing more self-control Helen steals sidelong glances at him, not openly smiling at him. She would like to show her face and her naked breasts, but her sense of decency reproves her and represses these full-blown excesses. A confused fear makes her heart beat unevenly. Paris senses this. He is on fire and full of daring. Love, that great maker of promises, produces signs of an easy prey as the signals give him hope, as the head nods appreciatively,

interpres cordisque vagi presentior index
leno oculus taciti garrit preludia voti.
ut vero explicitas peregrini Tindaris auri 245
blandicias hausit complutaque murice vela
conspexit, quid agat heret, prebere rogatas
prompta manus cogique volens. at turba precandi
stipatrix iuveni fas invidet. inclite predo,
ne propera! dabit illa manus, manus aurea vincet. 250
plus opibus, minus ore potes. Cicerone secundo
non opus est, ubi fantur opes. quin ipsa rapinis
blanditur Fortuna tuis: urbs, aura, Lacena,
nuda, favens, facilis ceptum iuvat. urbis Helea
nomen. in hanc pelagus undis declivibus actum 255
proxima litoreis delambit tecta procellis
et medias impingit aquas clauditque profundo.
hic Latonigenis cognatas struxerat aras
prisca fides. iubet hic noctem regina propinquam
excubiis hilarare sacris, templum ipsa superbum 260
prima petit solitoque deos implorat honore.
res cupido perlata Frigi, temeraria sancit
consilia indulgetque aditus in vota secundos
pollicito maiore Venus. rapere haut mora nuptam
victor et imbelles populari destinat aras. 265
tantaque precipitem pulsat lascivia mentem,
vix noctem exspectat suspenso vespere credens
zelotipum Titana suis livere secundis.

and the seducing eye, that spokesman and more immediate sign of
a flighty heart, speaks the prelude of an unspoken desire. As soon
45 as Helen took in the ostentatious delights of the foreign gold and
saw the sails steeped in purple, she no longer knows what to do,
being ready to touch hands if asked and yet wanting to be forced.
50 But the packed crowd prevents the young prince from asking. Do
not be too hasty, famous pirate! She will give you her hand: your
golden hand will win. Your wealth can achieve more than your tongue.
There is no need for Cicero on your side when wealth is speaking.
Why, even Fortune herself favours your acts of abduction: the empty
city, the favourable breeze and the complaisant Helen all help your
55 enterprise. The name of the city is Helea. The sea is driven into
it by towering waves in stormy weather, beating against the houses
nearest the shore, swirling about and covering them with water.
Here the ancient religion had built similar altars for Phoebus and
Diana. Queen Helen gives orders that the following night should be
60 celebrated here with holy vigils. She is the first to go to the
superb temple to pray to the gods with the usual reverence. Her
action is reported to the lustful Trojan. Venus approves his rash
plan, affording him easy access to his desire with an even greater
promise. He decides there and then to abduct the wife of Menelaus
65 and to plunder the peaceful altars like a conqueror. And so great
is the lust that drives his rash thoughts he can hardly wait for
nightfall, believing that the jealous sun was prolonging the
evening, envious of his successes.

Raptus Helene

Fregerat Hesperias radiis languentibus undas
Phebus et astrorum medio poscebat in alto 270
nauta diem; tellus, aer, mare celsa remenso
consopita deo, strepitu defuncta silebant
undique et in teneros nutabant ocia sompnos.
at Paris obsequio noctis presentius audet
inpaciens differre deos, Veneremque secutus 275
primus ad inbelles thiasos et debile vulgus
armatum maturat iter, ludentia turbat
fana ferox. non, hospes, Hymen, non coniuga sacra,
hospicii non obstat honos, non ultor iniqui
asperior tutela deus? temere omnia preceps 280
aspernata Venus, nil respectura decorum
in facinus votumque ruit. rapit ergo Lacenam
tendentemque manus et leta fronte vocantem
Dardanus aut rapitur potius. gratare tropheis,
predo, tuis, agnosce deos! post aspera multa 285
excidium lucratus abis revehisque parenti
quas nollet peperisse faces. heu, perdite, nescis
quas tecum clades, quantos fugiente tumultus
classe refers. tuque, Herculea corruptior unda,
Bellorofonteo flagrantior igne, sereno 290
certa minus, thalamos linquis, Ledea, iugales
et spreto tociens iterum querenda marito
numquam rapta fugis. nunc, o Lilibea vorago,
latratus Siculi, Libicus tenor et quod in omni
sevit triste mari mixtis huc confluat undis, 295
has infestet aquas primosque ultrice procella

The Abduction of Helen

The sun had broken through the western waves with his dying rays and in the middle of the deep the sailor was calling for the light of the stars. The earth, the sky and the sea, after being put to rest by the god who had gone through the heavens, all lay silent, bereft of noise. Everywhere repose nodded off into gentle sleep. But with the aid of darkness Paris is more confident and daring, not bearing to delay his destiny, and following Venus, he leads the way quickly under arms to the peaceful celebrations of the gentle sex. He turns the festive temple into wild uproar. O guest, does not Hymen or the sanctity of marriage or the honour granted you as a visitor stand in your way? Or even the god that avenges evil, a harsh protector indeed? Venus rashly spurns everything in her headlong rush. She will have no regard for civilised behaviour as she hastens to her lust for sin. So Trojan Paris snatches Helen as she holds out her hands, encouraging him with her happy expression - or rather Paris is snatched by her. Congratulate your spoils, pirate, and acknowledge the favour of the gods! After many a hardship you leave with the reward of destruction and carry back to your mother the firebrands she did not want to give birth to. Alas, you are doomed. You do not know what disasters, what great wars you are taking home with you in your hit-and-run fleet. And you, Helen, daughter of Leda, more venomous than the marsh Hercules dried up, more torrid than the fire breathed on Bellerophon, less reliable than fair weather, you are leaving your marriage bed. Again and again you will be sought by the husband you abandoned. You are running away, never abducted! Now may Charybdis and Scylla and the Syrtes and whatever rages grimly in any sea flow here with united force and infest these waters. With avenging storm

amplexus medium solvat mare! multa nocentes
mutat, si vetitis velox occurrerit ausis.

Postquam exempta quies et mesto pulsa fragore
inscia turbatas hausere silentia voces, 300
aure prius mensi, fremitus ubi et unde tumultus,
armati cognata petunt oracula cives.
hic tritas stridere liras, hic pocula cernunt
effuso calcata deo, funalia lucem
ponere et effracto lacrimari lampada vitro. 305
mirati, qua clade nova iocunda sileret
relligio, que causa pios inopina tumultus
flexerit, advertunt alias ad litora lites
et toto sonuisse mari: 'quo, perfide leno,
hospicii temerator, abis? sic digna rependis, 310
regales predate thoros'? hiis nobile vulgus
excitum arma fremit raptaque superstite turba
invadunt Frigios. illi nec pandere vela
molirique fugam cessant nec iungere bello
dignantur dextras contempta paupere pugna. 315
sola tamen tumidos pertemptat gloria captis
iniectare manus, proprium cum quisque tropheum
ostentare paret aut cive aut virgine rapta.

Reditus Paridis

Ecce redit Paphie meritus virgulta corone
victrices vinctura comas Tenedoque potitus 320
iam minus audentem solatur predo Lacenam,
iam tandem patrie memorem. sed gnarus adulter

may the middle of the ocean break their first embraces! Harsh punishment affects the guilty when it has speedily come upon forbidden sins.

After the calm has been broken and expelled by the sad tumult, the silence in its ignorance absorbed the troubled sounds. Armed citizens make for the connected altars after first listening to where the noise and uproar were coming from. Here they see smashed lyres squeaking, goblets trampled on and the wine spilled, chandeliers shedding their candles, lamps dripping oil from their broken glass globes. Wondering what unknown disaster had caused the joyous religious ceremony to become silent, what unexpected event had stopped the holy songs, they realise that there are other struggles going on at the beach and over the whole of the sea the cry was ringing out: 'Where are you going, treacherous lecher, violater of hospitality? Is this how you repay courtesy, by plundering a royal bed?' Aroused by these words the noble mob clatter their weapons. Joining up with the surviving crowd they attack the Trojans. These, however, do not stop spreading their sails in preparation for escape, not deigning to join battle in their scorn for such a small force. Glory alone finally persuades them to lay their proud hands on captives as each prepares to exhibit his own trophy by grabbing some man or girl.

The Return of Paris

See, now Paris returns, having earned the shoots of the myrtle crown of Venus to bind his hair in victory. Putting in at Tenedos the pirate consoles Helen who is now less bold and at last thinking of her homeland. But the clever adulterer

polliicitis fluxum meche sancire favorem
et fictos lenire metus, ebur aggerat Indum,
thura Sabea, Mide fluvios et vellera Serum. 325
ac mundi maioris opes, quodque educat aer
iocundum, pontus clarum vel fertile tellus,
hec faciles emere thoros, domuere rebelles
amplexus, pepigere fidem. non iam oscula reddit,
non reddenda negat Helene, sed pectore toto 330
incumbens gremium solvit, premit ore, latentem
furatur Venerem, iamque exspirante Dione
conscia secretos testatur purpura rores.
proh scelus! an tantis potuisti, pessima, votis
indulsisse moras exspectabatque voluptas 335
emptorem? o teneri miranda potentia sexus!
precipitem in lucrum suspendit femina luxum
nec nisi conducto dignatur gaudia risu.

Res hilarat vulgata Friges, Priamoque sereni
clarescunt vultus, rugas rarescere sentit 340
infelix animi morbus dolor, improba paulum
cedit hiems mentis, voto dux augure sperat
reddendam Hesionen, Helenam si reddat Achivis.
nondum Segeas portu digressus harenas
Dardanus attigerat, meritos mentita triumphos 345
obvia pompa subit. pars curru vecta superbo
aerium suspendit iter, pars cetera casum
haut metuens gressu vestigia paupere texit
obsequio contenta pedum, et - que cura novorum! -
Inachiam visura nurum plebs currit hanela 350

stabilises the fickle favours of the whore with promises,
soothing her imagined fears. He adds Indian ivory,
Arabian incense, rivers of gold and Chinese silk. The
riches of Asia, whatever delights the sky or the clear sea or
the fertile earth produce, all these bought an easy seduction,
overcame any resistance to his embraces and guaranteed her fidelity.
Helen now not only kisses him first but does not hold back if
kissed first. Lying on him with her whole body, she opens her
legs, presses him with her mouth and robs him of his semen. And
as his ardour abates the purple bedlinen that was privy to their sin
bears witness to his unseen dew. What evil! O wicked woman, were
you able to put a check on such passionate desire? Was your lust
waiting for a purchaser? What marvellous power in the gentle sex!
Woman holds back her precipitate lust to obtain wealth and does
not deign to give joy unless her smile has been paid for!

When the news is known it cheers up the Trojans. Priam's expressions
becomes serenely happy. Grief, that unhappy illness of the mind feels
its wrinkles diminish and the harsh winter of his thoughts recedes a
little as he uses his prayers as an augur, hoping that Hesione will be
returned if he returns Helen to the Greeks. Paris had left the harbour
but had not yet reached the Sigean shore. A procession sets out to
meet him in the mistaken belief that he deserved the triumph. Some,
riding in splendid chariots, go along high in the air, while others,
not fearing a fall, wend their way like the poor, content with the
aid of their feet. Always lovers of novelty, the ordinary people
run quickly to see the young Greek bride,

contemptrix opere, nutricis et immemor artis
nec lucri meminit, predam dum spectet amenam.
at cui sublimes humeros proceraque colla
invidit natura brevis, vel desuper altis
incumbit tectis vel recto calce fatigat 355
articulos humilesque gradus suspendit in altum.
hoc populo dederat vulgati fama decoris
certamen mirandi Helenam. subit illa pudice
ora gerens, oculis nusquam vaga, voce faventi
spectantum pudibunda parum mixtoque nitore 360
sidereas neutrata genas.

Vaticinium Cassandre

At regia vates
ut venisse Parim certo Cassandra relatu
audit et adductam monstrum fatale Lacenam,
ad tripodas questura fugit ramosque loquaces
ore premit poscensque deum non irrita longum 365
fatis plena redit. claretque interprete vultu
extorti vindicta dei, furiosa potestas
imbelles vexat artus. cervice rotata,
crine umbrante humeros, oculis spargentibus ignem
et facie perdente fidem nunc livida vitrum, 370
nunc flammata facem superat, nunc pallida buxum.
tali se mediis procerum tot milibus infert
ore furens tremulosque gradus vix ebria figit
atque ita Tindaridem cernens: 'tune illa iuvenca,
que saltus ingressa novos presepe paternum 375
incesta liquisse fuga taurumque iugalem

with scant regard for their work. They forget the skill that feeds them. They even forget money as they gaze at the plundered beauty. Those whose short stature begrudged them high shoulders and long
55 necks either look down from high roofs or stand with raised heels, making their toes ache as they hoist their lowly stance. The reputation of her beauty that had been spread about had made the
60 people struggle to admire Helen. She walks along to the applause of the spectators, looking modest and keeping her gaze fixed, although blushing a little, so that her face is neither white nor red, but a blend of both.

The Prophecy of Cassandra

As soon as she heard for certain that Paris had returned and had brought back Helen, the fatal portent, Cassandra, the royal prophetess, rushes to the tripods to complain. She interrogates the talking laurel
65 branches, and not having to wait unanswered for long when she calls the god, she returns filled with the future. The vengeance of the god she had taken by force appears in her prophetic face while his imperious power shakes her gentle limbs. Her neck rolls about, her hair covers
70 her shoulders, her eyes flash sparks. As her face changes its appearance it is now greener than glass, now redder than a torch, now paler than boxwood. With such a face she enters madly into the middle of many thousands of nobles, hardly able to walk properly as she is under the influence. Catching sight of Helen she says:
75 'Are you the heifer that is said to have entered new pastures, leaving your father's manger in sinful flight and the bull you mate with

diceris et nostros petis importuna maritos?
ite, viri, deus "ite" iubet, pontoque vel igne
maternas abolete faces, ne dira sequatur,
quam cecini, clades!" sic paucis questa quiescit, 380
expediuntque deum suspiria longa relictum.

Hiis hilares herent animi, totusque faventum
sopitur fremitus. favissent agmina vatis
imperio! motas reverentia principis iras
obruit indignisque datur Cassandra catenis. 385
rex Helenam lenit inopinaque probra gementis
solatur blandus suspiria; vatis hanelas
excusat Furias celeresque ad iurgia voces
et vicio capitis solitos sevire tumultus.
nec mora, sollempni lascivit regia cultu 390
imperiis ornata ducis tedasque pudendas
tollit adulter Hymen. melius caligo profunda
pollutum mersisset opus! quid nomine sacro
incestum phalerare iuvat? pretendit operta
bracteolam caries, agnum lupus, ulcera bissum, 395
sed Famam fraus nulla latet. non una duorum
esse potest; nam prima fidem dum federa debent,
alterius non uxor erit, sed preda cubilis.

Apparatus Grecorum ad bellum

Interea Graium preceps perlabitur orbem
luctus et Europe dotatas nomine terras 400
armato rumore quatit. leduntur in uno
una omnes, seu quod populos iniuria regum

to seek a husband amongst us, you ruthless creature? Go on, men. The god commands it. By fire or water destroy the mother's firebrands lest the tragic disaster I foretold should follow!' After uttering this brief complaint she falls silent. Long sighs show clearly that the god has left.

The Trojans' happy spirits falter at these words and all the noisy applause dies down. The crowd would have obeyed the order of the prophetess, but respect for King Priam crushes the anger Cassandra had aroused and she is unjustly clapped in chains. The king consoles Helen and kindly calms her sighs as she bewails the unexpected insults. He excuses the gasping frenzy of the prophetess, her words that quickly become quarrelsome, her tendency to rant and rage, putting it all down to insanity. In no time at all the palace is resplendent in festive splendour, decorated at the king's command. Adulterous Hymen lifts high the shameful marriage torches. It would have been better if deep darkness had buried this dishonourable deed! What is the good of dressing up adultery in a holy name? Hidden dry rot hides itself under gold leaf, the wolf under the guise of a sheep, a running sore under fine linen, but no deceit can escape Rumour. One woman cannot belong to two husbands; for while her first vows have validity she will not be the wife of another, only his bedroom spoils.

The Greek Preparations for War

Meanwhile grief spreads quickly through the Greek-speaking world, shaking the lands of Europe with rumour of war. Everyone is affected by what happened to Menelaus, whether because an injury inflicted on a king

acrius incendit, seu regnis prelia livor
inducit, seu quisque suas presumit in iras,
quod fieri sibi triste potest; quod flere peractum 405
quodque pati potuere, gemunt. hinc omnibus idem,
idem animus similes scelerum precidere motus
et thalamos sancire metu. ruit ocius ergo
nec iussa exspectat populus, belli ardor inerti
nascitur, augetur forti, sic prelia vulgus 410
precipit. at viduos it solatura Penates
clara ducum series, Malee quos erigit umbo,
quos Larissa fovet, quos cetera Grecia nutrit.
enumerem facilesque fide dictante meatus
ultrices Danaum certo sequar ordine vires, 415
que loca, qui reges, pelagus quot quisque fatiget
classibus? at celebres hac novi parte Camenas
fraudari titulis auresque offendere molles.
pauca tamen studio non egrescente faventum
succincte dixisse velim numerique sigillo 420
iuratas signare rates: fert bella bis una,
bis centum et decies centum, quas undique raptas
Cicropii vocat unda sinus et Apollinis equor.
huc acies, huc arma meant, hinc bellica classis
ordiri disponit iter, sic culmen herile 425
imperii iussit, statuit consulta potestas.

Submersio Castoris et Pollucis

Ast ubi gesta Frigum geminos vulgata Lacones
concussere, fremunt ambo, dolor excitat ambos,
ambos ira quatit. non sic orbata leones

arouses people more keenly or because envy brings war to empires or
because everyone takes personal umbrage at something cruel that might
05 happen to oneself. They all bemoan what they could lament when done
and what they might have had to suffer. And so they were all of
one mind on this point, that is to cut short any similar impulses
to crime and to make marriage inviolable through fear. Thus
the people move quickly without waiting for orders. The
10 desire for war is born in the cowardly and increased in the
brave - in this fashion did the ordinary people anticipate
battle. But a succession of famous leaders goes to offer
condolence to the bereaved household, coming from Mount Malea, Larissa
and the rest of Greece. Should I enumerate and list the avenging
15 Greek powers in hallowed order, with truth dictating the easy path,
telling what were the places, who were the leaders and how many ships
they each had to burden the sea? But I know that it is in this part
that several poetic muses lost their reputations and gave offence to
sensitive ears. However I would like to make some brief comments
20 without the enthusiasm of my supporters waning, and to stamp with the
seal of number the federation of ships. One thousand two hundred and
two ships go to war, summoned from everywhere to the bay of Athens
and the docks protected by Apollo. It is on here that the armies and
25 weapons converge, from here that the battle fleet decides to begin
its journey. Thus the noble supremos ordered, thus the power-making
council decided.

The Drowning of Castor and Pollux

But when the deeds of the Trojans were recounted to Castor and Pollux,
they are shaken. Both rage, aroused by grief and moved by anger.

lustra indignati lugent, non fulminis ales 430
sic gemit elinguis inopina silentia nidi.
haut mora, conscendunt classem Lesboque relicta,
dum preceps animus et nil decoctius audet
ira recens, nullos exspectatura sequentes
haurit iter fluidum pietas memor. alta tenebat 435
Castor, et Iliacas iam iam poscebat harenas
excidium latura ratis. nox obviat atra
defensura Friges armatique aeris ira
instrepit et geminis expugnat vela procellis.
o pietas, qua nulla Deum presentius ambit 440
virtus! o mitis fraterni candor amoris!
sola hec in geminos cessit discordia fratres,
discordes habuisse metus; hic illius, ille
huius fata timet, quotiensque illabitur equor
invergitque latus puppis subitura profundum, 445
equoris occursum certatim vertice prono
anticipare parant et sic proclamat uterque:
'in me, dira Thetis, in me, sevissime Triton,
has intende minas, tantos molire tumultus;
hunc serves, huic parce, precor'. tandem acrius aucto 450
incumbente Notho nil iam sperante carina
Ledei iuvenes nexis per colla lacertis
nata simul simili deponunt corpora fato.

Desine, Cicropii funesta licentia pagi,
incestos generare deos! non fabula celum, 455
sed virtus non ficta dabit. quos cecus ab alto
mersit in ima furor, in summos erigis axes

Angry lions do not mourn their plundered dens in this way, nor does the bird of Jupiter bemoan the unexpected silence of the tongueless nest. Without delay they board ship and leave Lesbos while their headstrong feelings and immediate anger dare something not premeditated. In brotherly love for their sister, without waiting for any followers they race across the sea, Castor steering straight ahead. The boat, intent on bringing destruction to the Trojans, was already making for the Trojan beach when darkness black as night intervenes in defence of the Trojans. The angry hostile sky roars and attacks their sails with its two-fold squalls. O piety! No virtue reaches more closely to God. O gentle sincerity of brotherly love! This was the only difference between the twins, namely of having different fears: Castor feared the death of Pollux, Pollux of Castor. Each time the sea breaks over the boat and the boat dips its side, as though going to the bottom, each strives by thrusting his head forward to take the brunt of the wave first, and each spoke thus: 'Against me, harsh Thetis, direct these threatening waters, against me, most cruel Triton, heap your huge seas. Preserve and spare him I pray!' But at last, as the south wind grows in strength, battering them more fiercely, and the ship is now in a helpless state, the young sons of Leda throw their arms around each other's neck and die together just as they had been born together.

O deadly licence of the Athenian world, cease from creating bastard gods! Myth will not give a place in Heaven - only true virtue can do that. Those whom blind fury of the sea has dashed from the heights to the depths, you, Athens, raise to the heights of Heaven

et similes Iovis esse iubes. quos ignis in auras,
in scopulos sparsit fluctus, mentiris adeptos
sidera gentilisque preces deludis acerre. 460
Tindaridis, quos hausit hiems, dans Attica celum
fabula Castoreos casus Pollucis in ortum
fingit et alterni redimit dispendia fati.
at neutrum testata deum feralis utrique
Atropos iniecit laqueum, quo fortibus egros, 465
quo sontes placidis, inopes quo regibus equat.
sola tamen Fatis Ledeum Lesbos amorem
concessisse negat raptosque secuta Lacones,
quos nec apud Frigios, mediis nec repperit undis,
credidit esse deos sterilique reversa favore 470
diis urbes auxit, thure aras, marmore templa.
sic Britonum ridenda fides et credulus error
Arturum exspectat exspectabitque perenne.

and command them to be like Jupiter. Those whom fire has scattered to the breezes and the waves have driven on to the rocks, you, in your lying fashion, say have attained the stars.
60 You deceive the prayers offered with pagan sacrifice. The storm swallowed up the sons of Tyndareus, yet the Attic myth puts them in Heaven, imagines the setting of Castor at the rising of Pollux
65 in order to make good the losses of their alternate mortality. But deadly Atropos, proving that neither was a god, imposed on each the snare of death which is the same for strong and weak, violent and gentle, paupers and kings. The men of Lesbos alone deny that these loving brothers had yielded to the fates; pursuing the lost pair they did not find them at Troy or on the sea, so
70 believed they were gods. Having returned to Lesbos, with useless devotion they increased the cities with gods, the altars with incense, the temples with marble. Just so is the laughable credulity and mistaken belief of the Britons who await the return of King Arthur now and will always go on doing so.

COMMENTARY

BOOK ONE

1. Iliadum lacrimas: Juv.10.261. Although Joseph is among those poets least likely to quote verbatim, it was normal practice to start a poem with a quotation from the Bible or from one of the *auctores* studied in the schools. He uses various synonyms for Troy or Trojan: only occasionally is one term used specifically.

2. two wars: referring to the first sacking of Troy by Hercules and the second by Agamemnon. For the Latin cf. Stat. *Theb*. 1.19. Like Juvenal, Statius was one of the most-studied classical authors in the Middle Ages. Several commentaries on their works are extant, testifying to their use in the schools. The zeugma involved is similar to that at the beginning of the work of another of Joseph's favourite authors, Lucan.

7. veri sacra fides: this circumlocution for veritas ('truth') is borrowed from Claud.*Bell.Get*.1.553. To this rhetorical feature is added another, namely prosopopeia or personalisation.

11. humble voice: while self-deprecation or 'humility topos' is another rhetorical feature regularly employed by medieval writers, its use here is particularly apposite in view of Joseph's plebeian birth.

14. laughter of the mob: this and several other derogatory references to the lower classes show that Joseph was unhappy about his origins.

15. contemporaries: the quarrel between the ancients and the moderns was very fierce in the 12th c. The inclusion of excerpts of Joseph along with other medieval writers in the *florilegia* of the 13th c. shows that the moderns won, though their victory was only temporary: cf. B. Stock, '*Antiqui* and *Moderni* as giants and dwarfs', *Modern Philology* 76 (1979), 370-73 and H.G. Rötzer *Traditionalität und Modernität* (1980) chs 4 and 5.

19. mento..mente: this example of paronomasia is also found in Walter of Châtillon's poem 'Ecce nectar roseum' in K. Strecker *Moralisch-Satirische Gedichte Walters von Châtillon* (Heidelberg, 1929) 14.4.4.

20. Youth *etc*: the use of *sententiae* ('maxims') was another common rhetorical device learned essentially through Terence and Lucan. Vernacular maxims were often translated into Latin hexameters.

25. Dares: Dares was supposed to have been an eye-witness of the second Trojan War and consequently a much more reliable source than Homer (i.e. the Latin *Ilias Latina*) or Virgil, both of whom lived centuries after the events!
28. Aware of the truth: it is typical of Joseph that in dismissing Virgil he should recall him verbally: *mens conscia veri* is obviously based on *mens conscia recti* (*Aen.*1.604).
30. Athenian Areopagus: Joseph uses *pagus* for *Areopagus* and an adjective based on Cecrops, the founder of Athens.
31. father: this reference to the spiritual title begins the dedication to Joseph's uncle Baldwin that was added later. See Introd. p.5.
    Canterbury: Baldwin was Archbishop of Canterbury from 1185 to 1190, succeeding Richard who was a very unsatisfactory holder of the See. For Richard cf. *Dictionary of National Biography* s.n.
33. third..dignity: to be Pope. This is not pure hyperbole on Joseph's part. Baldwin had already been proposed for the cardinalate in 1178 by the Pope's legate in France, a man of great influence. Furthermore, Baldwin had become a Cistercian monk, leaving Exeter to become Abbot of Ford, and from St Bernard's time onwards the influence of the Cistercians at Rome was very powerful. Baldwin was also well-known as a writer.
34. Worcester: Baldwin was Bishop of Worcester from 1180 to 1185.
38. third after Thomas: in fact in our reckoning he was second. Thomas Becket was followed by Richard and Baldwin.
    second Thomas: I can see no justification in assuming, as Gompf does (e.g. 20, 38), that this means that his name was Thomas Baldwin. He is a second Thomas because, like Becket, he was a worthy holder of the See of Canterbury. Lines 38-39 once contained a reference overtly critical of Richard that Joseph appears to have dropped when he revised his text. For *alter/sol oriens, rebus successor, moribus heres* AP read *una/discrevit geminum nox interiecta serenum*. The glossators AP have both readings.
40. honour: this cryptic phrase appears to be a conflation of Psalm 48.13 and Genesis 3.19, meaning that unlike man, the rise of honour does not necessarily entail a return to its origins.
42. fortune: Joseph appears to have in mind Juv.7.197-98.

43. top..bottom: the image here is of the medieval wheel of fortune with its four positions *regno - regnavi - sum sine regno - regnaturus*.
44. cease: Joseph is attacking priests like Richard.
50. you: Baldwin.
52. father..priest: Becket.
54. share: Joseph seems to have in mind a situation similar to that which obtained in the royal family after the king, Henry II, appointed his eldest son as co-king, calling him Henry III. The young Henry died in 1183, six years before his father, so is never counted among the kings of England.
55. O mighty one: for some inexplicable reason Bezzola thinks that either Henry II or Richard I is meant, but Joseph is obviously still addressing Baldwin.
57. holy armies..greater song: a reference to the Third Crusade and Joseph's epic *Antiocheis*.
59. fame..worldwide: the influence for this thought is Lucan's apostrophe to Caesar (4.298).
64. bride: Medea. The reference is to Jason's expedition to Colchis to obtain the Golden Fleece, which succeeded because of Medea who left with Jason. Joseph's source is Dares 1. For medieval knowledge of the story see F.A. Dominguez, *The Medieval Argonautica* (Potomac, 1979).
65. Pluto: note how Joseph uses his Roman name, Dis, which is associated with wealth, and places it next to *opes* in the line. A further pun is present in his use of *egeste* meaning 'drawn out (of the earth) which is virtually a homonym of *egestas* meaning 'poverty'.
72. Golden Fleece: Joseph actually calls it the 'Phryxean sheep' using Ovid's phrase from *Her*.12.8. Phryxus escaped with his sister Helle from his stepmother Ino by flying on the back of a ram whose fleece was golden. When he arrived in Colchis he dedicated the ram to Mars. Joseph would have known the story through e.g. Ovid *Met*.4 or *Her*.18, Hyginus 3, or Vat. Myth.1.23.
74. dukes: I have taken the liberty of translating thus because Joseph probably thought in feudal terms. Peleus and Telamon would not have been so important as Hercules and Jason.
79. lap of Thetis: the sea. Thetis, a sea goddess, is used for the sea as this enables Joseph to insist on the sexual imagery of the first boat taking the sea's virginity. The imagery is re-inforced by the use of *pinus* as a phallic symbol linked to *penis* by paronomasia. See further

1.157-58. According to the A glossator *Tetios* is the genitive used when the sea is meant, *Tetidis* when it is the mother of Achilles, a remark which may reflect the confusion among mythologists of Tethys with her granddaughter Thetis.

80. ramis..remos: paronomasia.

83. gods bobbing: a reference to the painted and sculpted figures of deities on prows of ships.

85. noble breasts: again Joseph uses sexual imagery. See 3.173-74 for further use of this image. The Argo did not have sails according to legend. For a different sexual image of sails see 1.115.

86. danger: Joseph means ships which are a danger to human life.

87. Mount Haemus: the forest of Diana from which the pine was taken was on Mt Haemus in Thessaly.

90. harm the gods with gold: in diminishing their majesty by making golden images of them. The idea may have come from Pers.2.69.
gold with rocks: by scraping on the rocks the gold pictures of the gods painted on the hulls of ships.

91. new guest: Jason.

95. rapit aura ratem: note the assonance.
wrecker: the Argo. Lucan 3.196-97 may be behind the thought.

99. Symplegades: two islands or rocks at the entrance of the Euxine Sea, sometimes called *Cyaneae*, thought by the ancients to move together to crush any boat passing through them. The glossators are very sceptical of this belief.

102. Atropos: of the three Fates or *Parcae* Atropos is the one who actually cuts the thread of man's life.

104. contemtus: medieval spelling for *contemptus*.

105. Ypotades: this patronymic Joseph probably found in Ovid, *Met*.14. Corus: for Caurus. Cf. Virg.*Geo*.3.356.

107. fear the creator of the gods: this thought is influenced by Stat.*Theb*.3.661.

116. At last: Dares 2.

119. Trojan: Joseph uses the name of the Sigean promontory.

127. hospes non hostis: At 1.435 however, the *hospes* has become *hostis*. Cf. Ovid *Her*.17.10.

131. every land is common: the thought comes from Statius, *Theb*.8.320.

133. phariseat: for the bold coining of this verb from *pharisaeus*, cf. Walter of Châtillon, *Alexandreis* 4.238.

144. tuba: for *vox*. Cf. John of Salisbury, *Policraticus* 8.23 for a similar use.
158. delinita: *quasi diceret deflorata* P glossator. The A glossator's text had *delenita* which he glosses '*placata*' (placated). The deflowering image is better suited to the rest of the line and recalls 1.79.
160. swift: the reading ought to be *Pagasea*, the adjective regularly used by classical writers to denote the Argo since it was thought to have been built or launched in Pagasa in Macedonia. Glossator A offers no explanation while glossator P thinks the ship was thus called either because of the head of Pegasus sculpted on it or else from the place. All MSS have *Pegasea* so I have assumed that is what Joseph wrote and consequently have tried to interpret the meaning he gave it. In all probability he would have got it from a faulty text of Ovid, e.g. *Met*.7.1. or Lucan 2.715.
174. Typhis: the helmsman of the Argo.
182. Why should I recount: this is the rhetorical device of actually saying what one says one is going to omit, though Joseph does tell the tale very elliptically. Aeetes, King of the Colchians, made Jason plough land with bulls of Mars he had tamed, sow the teeth of a serpent as seeds, fight with the armed men who grew from the seeds and then kill the dragon guarding the Golden Fleece. The fire refers to the bulls that breathed flames from their nostrils, the courage is Jason's, the sword refers to the armed men who grew up.
189. procul..profani: based on Virg.*Aen*.6.258.
195. deaths: Joseph uses the name of the Fate who cuts the thread of life. Cf. 102n.
197. Memphis: stands for Egypt.
208. Salamina: the A glossator takes Joseph to task here, pointing out that the nominative should be *Salamis* and that the form *Salamina* is accusative as proved by Lucan 3.183, but Joseph is probably working from the accusative *Salaminam* in Hyg.24.
209. Terauneis: the reading should be *Therapneis* as in Stat. *Theb*.7.793, but presumably Joseph's source was defective. The glossators knew that it is a place name referring to Castor and Pollux but they appear to be unaware of the origin and have defective readings themselves. Leda was the mother of Castor and Pollux, Helen and Clytemnestra.
Orithyia: her Ismarian sons were Zetus and Calais, born to Boreas, King of Thrace, in whose country the mountain of Ismarus was to be found. Again it looks as if Joseph's

source was defective as he writes *Orithia*.

210. Calydonian mother: this cryptic phrase refers to the story of Althaea, wife of Oeneus, who caused the death of her son, Meleager, when he had killed his mother's two brothers. Joseph would have known the story from Ovid, *Met*.8. The expression 'not yet merely a sister' is a little puzzling as she ceased to be a sister before ceasing to be a mother, but presumably it refers to her acting more like a sister than a mother in causing Meleager's death.

214. Peloponensus: like the glossators Joseph obviously thought that the Peloponese was the name of Pelias' city.

224. O gods..O Fates..O chance: Joseph includes all three theories of the governing of human life in Pelias' complaint.

233. Did I want: this technique of question and answer in the same hexameter was taught in the schools.

238. Cf. Ovid, *Met*.7.518. Joseph uses another variation at 3.130.

240. three tyrants: Jupiter, Pluto and Neptune.

249. A banquet: see also the description of Hesione's wedding feast, 2.76-154. The idea presumably came to him from Dido's banquet for Aeneas (*Aen*.1.695ff).

255. Note the alliteration in this and the next line.

258. Joseph does not name Bacchus, but uses the circumlocution 'the god, the sweet go-between'. The context and the later reference to Bacchus in 263 warrant this interpretation.

264ff. In his complicated, involved fashion Joseph is saying in three different ways that the king was showing affection in offering so much varied food which effort had obtained. This is the rhetorical figure of *Interpretatio*: cf. Faral (1962^2) 277.

268. Dares 3.

270. Hercules' complaint refers cryptically to the events surrounding his birth. Alcmena, wife of Amphitryon, gave birth to twins, Iphiclus (son of Amphitryon) and Hercules (son of Jupiter). As Jupiter had boasted about the birth of his son, his jealous wife Juno sent two serpents down from heaven to see which son was his. When the serpents came to Iphiclus' cradle he cried. When they came to Hercules' he strangled them, so that, according to Joseph, they 'cried like a child'. At least, that seems to be Joseph's meaning, but I can find no version of the story that suggests that Hercules also cried. Cf. Vat.Myth.1.50.

276. Iunonior: for the bold coining of this comparative adjective which the glossators define as '*novercatior*' (more stepmotherish') cf. many similar examples from the 12th c.,

e.g. *ursior, tigridior*. See Sedgwick (1928), 359, Raby 2.164, Faral (1962[2]) 348. Sedgwick's emendation, (1930), 52, to *novercalior* is unjustified.

282. Eurystheus: he was the instigator of the twelve labours of Hercules through the machinations of Juno.

283. Lerna: killing the many-headed hydra of Lerna is usually regarded as Hercules' second labour but the order of the labours is not the same in all accounts. Cf. Vat.Myth.1.62 and Ovid, *Met*.9.
Cerberus: for his twelfth labour Hercules dragged Cerberus out of hell and forced him to spit out his venom on the rocks of Dodona, thus producing the flower *aconitum*. Cf. Ovid, *Met*.9 and Vat.Myth.1.57.

285. Antaeus: not one of Hercules' labours. He was a Libyan giant that Hercules fought who regained his strength every time he touched the ground, so Hercules had to hold him in the air until he squeezed him to death. Joseph could have known this story from one of a number of sources, e.g. Ovid, *Met*.9, Vat.Myth.1.55, Hyginus 31, Lucan 4.598ff, Stat.*Theb*.6.893 or Juv.3.88.

286. Rea: is obviously used for Antaeus' mother, Terra or Earth. Rea is strictly the daughter of Terra, but the two were regularly confused by mythologists.

289. depotuisse: *nil potuisse*.

292. Pergamum: the references are to Laomedon's perjury in refusing Apollo and Neptune the sum of gold he had promised them for building Troy's walls and his refusal to allow the Argonauts to stop over at Troy.

294. liquidoque Iovi: circumlocution for Neptune.

299ff. leader of the herd: a bull. The simile is based on Lucan 2.601-07.

300. lunatum robur: the shape of the new moon with its two horns lies behind this image.

304. thorus: the flesh around the bull's neck is used here to denote strength.

317. bugle: probably based on *Aen*.6.165, but both glossators think Joseph has money in mind.

318. mob: Joseph's anti-lower class feelings come to the fore again.

341. Simois: a river in Phrygia where much of the fighting took place during the war.

342. Peleus..Thetis: Joseph omits both names. Thetis married Peleus after Jupiter lost interest in her when he learned that any son born to her would be greater than the father. The usual story is that she was very reluctant to accept a

mortal husband after receiving the attentions of fellow gods, but Joseph seems to be following a different version. Likely sources, such as the *Excidium Troie*, Vat.Myth.1, 2, and 3, or Hyginus, make no mention of any reluctance on Thetis' part. Ovid, *Met*.11.221-65 suggests that she was not happy to have Peleus for a husband but does not mention a wedding nor any preference for a god.

346. prejudicial to his fates: because it would result ultimately in the death of his son, Achilles.
347. A similar line is found in Dracontius (8.127): *Dorica castra fremunt, iam Pergama vexat Achilles.*
348. equale..fulmen: variation on Aen.6.842.
     Ajax: three Ajaxes feature in this poem: Telamonian Ajax here; Locrian (or son of Oileus) in Books 4, 5 and 6; son of Nauplius in Book 6.
363. Joseph has ingeniously modified the Mars - Vulcan - Venus triangle (which he refers to in its normal context at 2.298-301) metaphorically to the fight in the sea, with Mars (warfare) and Vulcan (fire) against the sea (Venus' birthplace). Vulcan is called Lennius (=Lemnius) from his residence on Lemnos. At 2.300-01 Joseph puns on *Lennius* and *lenius*.
365. This line is a variation of Lucan 2.713.
368. dogs of Scylla: Joseph's conceit here appears to have caused confusion among his glossators. Both contain a statement that Scylla is a sea-monster whose top half is a woman and bottom half a dog (which explains why the waves are barking at 369), but whereas P does not gloss *Scilleos..canes* or mention the fact that Scylla was actually a rock, A says that the dogs are fish living near Scylla and then adds the detail that the barking waves are caused by the sound of the water entering cavities in the rock. Neither discusses the *monstra* at 370. Unlike the glossators, Joseph envisages that there are several dogs of Scylla that leave the Gulf of Sicily to come to Troy. It is salutary to note that *latrantibus undis* is found in Silius Italicus (3.471) which Joseph could not have known. Writers like Joseph could create striking phrases without the help of their predecessors.
372. Nereus: a god of the sea, father of the Nereids.
374. urnam: sea- and river-gods are often depicted holding an urn.
377. Atlas: Joseph seems to envisage Mt Atlas as a barrier separating the Mediterranean from the Atlantic.
379. first insult: the journey of the Argonauts was the first

insult inflicted on the sea-gods, but it had to be borne because it was written in the Fates. However, there was no valid reason for their putting up with the present insults.

381. steams: as so much hot human blood is being spilled in the sea the temperature of the water is rising towards boiling-point!
Charybdis: it is difficult to know why Joseph has brought Charybdis into this account unless he is suggesting that somehow it came into existence because of Scylla's success in feeding on mankind. The glossators are silent here.

385. model for criminality: theft in respect of the Golden Fleece, murder in respect of Hercules' attack on Troy.

386. This *sententia* conveys the same message as 3.297. For the source see Ecclesiasticus 8.11.

387. I take *Iliace manus* to refer to the Trojan people in general as distinct from the *Dardana pubes*, but they may be identical.

389ff. 'Thoughts come crowding on each other in such profusion that language is left panting behind' (Sedgwick (1930), 53-54) is a view that might well express what is going on here. Joseph is suggesting that war based on ambition is not as fierce as this which is based on anger and threats, and even though their rage has not been stimulated by their wounds, nevertheless it is just as fierce as if it had been because of the hatred that was present in the hearts of both sides.

391. cruda: = *crudelia*. Cf. Lucan 4.710 and Walter of Châtillon *Alexandreis* 1.147.

394. horse: Joseph sees the fighting in terms of medieval warfare. Peleus is a knight. At 401-02 Troy is surrounded by a moat. The fighting is a medieval attack on a moated castle with Telamon as a sapper. When Priam rebuilds the city one gate will have a portcullis (490), while all the nobles will have houses with towers and turrets.

395. Peleus ironically refers to the hospitality that Laomedon refused to offer the Argonauts. The idea of simply knocking on the door and it will be opened comes from the Gospel of St Matthew 7.7.

397. instare: historic infinitive for *instabant*.

408ff. The defence of the city is very medieval.

410. Dimus: the name of a Greek soldier, possibly based on Dymas, the Trojan killed by his fellow Trojans because he was disguised as a Greek (*Aen.*2.340 and 428), or on Dymnus, one of Alexander's officers (Quintus Curtius 6.7. and *Alexandreis* 3.65).

412. decalvavere: Joseph uses this biblical word to describe the removal of hair and beard.
420. grim voice: no help is given by the glossators in identifying this mysterious speaker.
431. Tirynthian: Hercules was often called this from the place he was supposedly brought up in.
454. Of Laomedon's four children named here only Hesione has any authority. Amphitus would appear to be borrowed from Ovid, *Met*.5 (a priest of Ceres). The A glossator, unhappy with the name, suggests Iphitus. There is an Iphitus associated with Hercules as an ally, not an enemy, and another, who is Trojan, in *Aen*.2. Volcontus probably derives from the *Excidium Troie* as a corruption of Volscens, the Latin chief who discovered Nisus and Euryalus in *Aen*.9. The error probably arose from the accusative *Vol(s)centem* being read as *Volcontum* and the nominative *Volcontus* formed from that. The variant readings in the *Excidium Troie* MSS are very diverse. Even in the Joseph MSS we find Vulcontus A, Volocontus O, Volentus P. I can find nothing plausible to explain Isiphilus, but that too is doubtlessly based on some corrupt text. Variant readings by scribes presumably trying to make some name that was known are Siphilus A, Sisiphus P.
458. A variation on Stat.*Theb*.9.556.
459. Dares 4.
461. Cf. Walter of Châtillon, *Alexandreis*, 1.390 and 3.27.
466. Lachesis: here stands for the Fates. She is the sister who spins the thread of life.
479ff. Although the language is Statian (e.g. *castigat*), the idea is from *Aen*.1.208-09.
482. Another *sententia* finishing a passage: cf. 386.
485. retribution: Joseph's use of Themesis is rather surprising. Nemesis would have been probable but the only evidence for it is the *editio princeps* where it surely is an emendation.
487. six entrances: cf. 6.131. Six gates of Troy are listed in Dares 4.
488ff. It is difficult to follow Joseph here. One would not expect a portcullis to cover only one gate of a pair.
492. lucro iactura fuit: variation on Stat.*Theb*.10.513.
497. Ylios: the name of the royal palace; Ylium is that of the city.
500. Phlegra: a reference to the valley in which the giants built a mountain to attack heaven and were defeated by Jupiter's thunderbolts.
citadels of the Assyrian virgin *etc*: a reference to the

tower of Babel whose construction on the orders of Semiramis was stopped by Jehovah with the confusion of languages. Cf. Genesis 11.7-8.

505. Cyclops: it was traditional to assert that any large construction had been built by the Cyclops.

508. Ucalegon: borrowed from *Aen*.2.312, where his house was set on fire by the Greeks. Joseph keeps the association of fire but has Ucalegon's house belching it out through the chimney, showing that he fully understood the practice of *imitatio*. Furthermore, whereas in the *Aeneid* Ucalegon was a respected elder here he will be among Troy's traitors. In Juv.3.199 he is simply a neighbour caught in a fire.

509. Antenor: Joseph is quietly preparing his character assassination of this man. Here he is one of the arrogant citizens of Troy; in Book 2 his embassy is forced on him and he allows his resentment to be seen by Telamon. After the embassy he will propose war and will be accused of coming to a secret personal arrangement with the Greeks. In Book 6 he will be the leader of the traitors and after the capture of Troy he will be installed as its new king.

510. limping Anchises: the anti-Virgilian mood continues with Joseph showing himself as clever as Virgil in using legends. Where Virgil had Aeneas carrying Anchises on his shoulders when leaving Troy because Anchises was too old to walk himself, Joseph refers obliquely to the cause of Anchises' limp and dislike of walking, his crippled feet. The legend was that after having had sexual intercourse with Venus Anchises boasted about it and was smitten by Jupiter's thunderbolt as a punishment. Out of affection for Anchises Venus averted the thunderbolt so that it only hit his feet. Cf. Vat.Myth.2.195. The versions in Hyginus 94, Vat.Myth.1.217 and Servius ad *Aen*.2.649 have slight variation of detail.

512. plaususque viarum: recalls the Virgilian *strata viarum* (*Aen*.1.422). Joseph actually uses *strata* at 6.176. Gompf cites *Aen*.8.717 as influential but fails to convince. Cf. also *Alexandreis* 4.175 *plana viarum*.

514ff. For this type of description with each noun having its accompanying adjective cf. Faral (1962[2]) 82. Here it is used as an epic catalogue. For earlier catalogues of trees cf. Ovid, *Met*.10.86ff, Virg.*Aen*.6.179ff, Stat.*Theb*.6.91ff, Claudian, *De Raptu Pros*. 2, 105ff. Chaucer followed Joseph in his *Parlement of Foules*, 177ff (cf. Root, 18).

515. sad cypress: because of its use in funeral pyres. Joseph uses it again at 6.868.

516. prophetic laurel: because of its use by Apollo in his oracle at Delphi.
travelling pine: ships were made of pine. Cf. Chaucer's 'sayling firr'.
517. conciliatory olive: the olive branch as a sign of peace.
hunting cornel: hunting spears were made of this wood.
bold ash: lances are made of ash.
518. companion: the vine. For the ancient use of elms as supports for the vine cf. Virg.*Geo*.1.2.
519. musical boxwood: because of its use in making musical instruments. Cf. Chaucer's 'boxtree piper'.
520. drunken vine: the vine itself, of course, is not drunken. Glossator A explains the use as *ab effectu*.
521ff. I have not found it possible to reproduce in English the sexual nature of Joseph's phrase.
522. Falernus: Falernian wine was often written about by the ancient poets. Falernus was in Campania.
524. another world: the Simois was said to rise on Mt Ida. For some reason Joseph thinks it rose elsewhere and travelled through many kingdoms before arriving in Phrygia.
532. Nereus: here used to denote the sea.
536. gave respite: as the following enumeration shows, so many gods had taken up residence in Troy or its surroundings that the heavens were significantly lighter, thus rendering Atlas' task that much easier.
544. fate of the city: the Palladium, a statue of Pallas, was kept in the citadel, and as long as it stayed there the Fates had decreed that Troy could not fall. It is referred to again, by Pallas herself, at 2.453, but then Joseph seems to forget about it. According to the legend Diomedes and Ulysses stole it.
546ff. Joseph's ingenuity is particularly inappropriately applied here to the description of an almost imperceptible mound!
548. non..nudi: this negative way of stating a fact is very characteristic of Lucan.
549. The negation continues. Joseph specifies that the 'genuine' regalia of Jupiter, his sceptre and thunderbolt, are found in Troy, not in Phoenicia where he was worshipped in the form of a bull nor in India where he was worshipped in the form of a ram. The information is both cryptic and gratuitous. The reference to the ram in India is an error found in Hyginus 133 and in Lactantius Placidus' commentary on Stat.*Theb*. at 3.476. At 3.71 Joseph gives the standard reference to Libya which he would have found in Lucan 9.510ff. or Ovid, *Met*.15.310.

BOOK TWO

1. <u>numerous children:</u> Priam was said to have 50 sons and 12 daughters, 17 of whom were born to Hecuba, his second wife, the rest to concubines.
2. <u>marriage:</u> his marriage to Hecuba was both happy and fruitful. His first wife, Arisba, was chosen for him by Laomedon, and he divorced her for Hecuba after Laomedon's death.
3. <u>permissible to remain blessed:</u> Joseph is again thinking of the wheel of fortune.
4. <u>Allecto:</u> Allecto is the Fury who carried out Juno's plans to cause the war between the Latins and the Trojans in *Aen.*7 and 10. Her presence at Troy seems to be Joseph's invention as well as her ambition to be Queen of Heaven. Joseph has transferred Juno's complaint in *Aen.*1 to Allecto.
5. <u>snakes:</u> the Furies were said to have whips of snakes or else snakes for hair. Cf. Vat.Myth.1.109 and 2.12.

15. Cf. Lucan 2.4.
22. <u>famous virgin:</u> Pallas.
24. <u>Gorgon's head:</u> according to both glossators Pallas had the image of the Gorgon's head painted on her shield. Whether this is something they had learned or whether they deduced it from *pretenta* is difficult to say. The usual localisation was on her breastplate, cf. Hyginus, *Poetica Astronomica*, 2.12, Vat.Myth. 2.39 and 112, 3.10. The holding out of the shield would suit Perseus better.
25. <u>Stygian Medusas:</u> the Furies of hell.
29. <u>Tisiphone:</u> she is the second of the Furies.
36. Cf. Ovid, *Her.*13.163.
41. <u>not a great disgrace:</u> the thought is that of Ovid, *Met.*9.5ff.
42. <u>humiles favor:</u> hypallage for *humilitas favorem*.
<u>exuo regem:</u> a bold variation on Stat.*Theb.*11.434.

43ff. All the examples quoted are of vanquished pleading with their victors. India and Bacchus refers to the celebrated story of Bacchus' expedition to the East where he defeated the Indians in a bloodless victory thanks to the use of wine, cf. Vat.Myth.2.80.

44. <u>Croesus with Cyrus:</u> Cyrus, King of Persia, defeated Croesus, King of Lydia, in 548 BC.
<u>Cyrus with Thamiris:</u> Thamiris (or Tomyris), Queen of the Massagetae, a Scythian tribe, defeated Cyrus in 530 BC. Joseph possibly knew the story from the Latin historian

Justinus who epitomised the history of Trogus Pompeius. Cyrus' life was written about by Xenophon in his *Cyropaedia*. Bale's statement that Joseph had written a Latin *Cyropaedia* (Introd. p.00) may have something to do with these lines. Cf. *Alexandreis* 2.526ff. and 5.389ff.

48. Erinis: Erinys for the Furies or Eumenides may possibly derive from Ovid, *Met*.4.490 or Virg.*Aen*.2.337.

51. leto: I have translated this as the ablative of *letum* 'death'. It could be the dative of *letus* (*laetus*) 'happy'. The presence of *leta* (*laeta*) two lines later offers little help in deciding which word Joseph intended as medieval writers employed both the technique of the same word in different cases and of paronomasia.

56. enemy I made: the eastern Phrygians he had attacked. Cf. Ovid, *Met*.5.94.

57. enemy made for me: the Greeks.

68. Dares 5.

70. Magnesia: home of Peleus.
Sparta: home of Castor and Pollux, twin sons of Tyndareus.

71. Pylos: home of Nestor.

73. Piliam..senectam: Martial 8.2.7.

74. Telamon the happy: because of his imminent wedding. His city is Salamis.

75. Lachesis: Joseph envisages Lachesis feeling sorry for those whose life-threads she had spun and looking for a way out to avert the inevitable.

76-187. The description of Hesione's wedding to Telamon appears to have no classical source though it certainly has Dido's banquet for Aeneas (*Aen*.1.697-756) as its inspiration - noise, singing, deep-drinking and the relatively rare word *lychni*. Joseph gives us a medieval wedding feast in classical dress. Cf. 1.248-97 for a similar meal.

77. purple..Tyrian ostentation: Cf. Hor. *Ep*.1.10.26 and Virg. *Aen*.4.137.

79. Juno: she was the goddess of marriage. Cf. her role in *Aen*.1 (with Aeolus) and 4 (with Dido). Also Vat.Myth.3.4.

81. ventripotens: this compound adjective, based on *omnipotens*, is similar in humour to Alcuin's description of a Dutch bishop as *vaccipotens* (4.7).

83. fecundam..sitim: this effective oxymoron is explained by glossator A '*quia bonum vinum sequentem fecit bibere*'. Cf. John of Hauville, *Architrenius*, 2.285 *fecundo fecunda mero facundia surgit*.

84. civiliter: glossed '*more civium quibus usus bibendi propensior est*', and therefore has nothing urbane or courtly about it, contrary to the prevailing fashion of Joseph's time. In Spanish Latin *civiliter* had a different derogatory meaning of 'cruelly', because of civil war: cf. J.E. López Pereira, 'Latín Medieval y filología hispana' *Verba* 10 (1983) 155-68. In the *Alexandreis* 1.180 and 195 Walter of Châtillon uses it to mean 'for the use of townspeople'.

88. The British nation was well-known for its drinking in the Middle Ages. The glosses note '*cui quasi per prerogativam attribuitur bibendi potentia*'. Contemporary texts such as Nigel Wireker's *Speculum Stultorum*, 1515-30 (esp. 1520 *fercula multiplicant et sine lege bibunt*), Geoffrey of Vinsauf's *Poetria Nova*, 1003 *potatrix Anglia*, Jacques de Vitry's *Historia Occidentalis* (p.279) *potatores Anglicos*, testify to the reputation of the British nation as heavy drinkers.

102. musician: I take this to refer to medieval dancing. *Alternat* indicates the presence of two sets of dancers, one male, the other female, that the musician leads out, but Joseph seems to have adapted the role of the *choraules* in Roman comedy (cf. the end of Plautus, *Stichus*, with *plaudite* in the last line). However, the 'applaud' of comedy becomes 'clap your hands' of the dance, and we probably have here the picture of a medieval *jongleur* in action. E. Faral, *Les Jongleurs en France*, (Paris, 1964[2]) gives several examples of their involvement with dances. See esp. the description of the 'Jeu du Chapelet' (p.233) and the quote from Theganus (p.273 no. 6a) '*procedant thymelici, scurri* (sic) *et mimi cum coraulis et citharistis*'. For the actual description of a dance cf. *Ruodlieb* 11.25-27.

104. Salamine: this genitive confirms that Joseph thought the nominative was *Salamina*. It is typical of Joseph that he makes the reader work hard, having associated Telamon with Salamis at 1.208, but leaving the link unmentioned at 2.74 where it would have been expected.

109ff. Joseph's song of praise for Hercules shows just how ingenious he can be. The idea of singing a song of praise at a banquet probably comes from *Aen.*1 where Iopas sings at the end of Dido's banquet for Aeneas. The choice of Hercules as subject is probably influenced by the celebration in honour of Hercules in *Aen.*8, while the actual material for the song is to be found for the most part in

Hercules' complaint to Juno as he perished (Ovid, *Met*.9.176-98).

113. his help: in referring to the battle of the Giants and the Gods at 2.371-91 Pallas makes no mention of Hercules' role. At 2.518-23 Venus casts doubt on Pallas' account but she does not mention Hercules. The accounts of the attacks on heaven are often confused in ancient writers, e.g. Vat.Myth.1 and 2. The attack of the Giants is associated strictly with Otos and Ephialtes who piled Ossa on Pelion in Phlegra according to Hyginus. He attributes their defeat to Apollo (28). Vat.Myth.2.55 attributes it to Jupiter's thunderbolt; neither mentions Hercules. At 1.500 Joseph names only Jupiter for the victory at Phlegra. Perhaps a commentary on Lucan at 6.347 gave Joseph his information. Vat.Myth.1.63 refers to the event very cryptically among what are called 'rare fables'.

117. exploit: by strangling the snakes Juno sent: cf. 1.270n.

118. scourge of Nemea: the Nemean lion that Hercules killed. Later he dressed in its skin.
Erymanthus: Hercules captured (here put to flight) the wild boar that was devastating the area of Erymanthus. Hyginus 30 says that Hercules slew it, but the glossators attribute its death to Theseus. However, it is likely that they are confusing the boar with the bull (see next note).

120. Crete from the bull: Hercules freed Crete from the bull that had gone berserk. It was the bull Pasiphae was enamoured of, later killed by Theseus. Cf. Vat.Myth.1.47 and 2.120.

121. Geryon..Cacus: the story has been compressed by Joseph into one line. Geryon was a Spanish monster king who owned large herds of cattle. Eurystheus sent Hercules to bring them back to Tiryns and when he was passing through Italy on his return journey some of the oxen were stolen and hidden by Cacus in his cave. Hercules was made aware of the loss by the lowing of the cattle and he killed Cacus in his cave. Cf. Vat.Myth.1.68 and 2.154 (where the compression is similar). Virg. *Aen*.8 is also to be considered. Ovid does not mention Cacus.

122. Hydra..Cerberus: see 1.283n.

123. Lapiths: I can find no reference to Hercules fighting the Lapiths. The glossators have no valid explanation either, but may have the answer indirectly. They state that the Lapiths were a people of Thessaly, sons of Ixion (one of whom was Pirithous) whom Hercules defeated, or else Centaurs, citing Claudian 34. 44 *prostratis maduit*

nubigenis Pholoe. According to Vat.Myth.1.61, citing Asper and Longus, Pholoe was a wood named after Pholus, a centaur who offered Hercules hospitality on his way to obtain the horses of Diomedes. A fight between Hercules and the Centaurs ensued, with Hercules the victor. It is conceivable that like the glossators Joseph thought Lapiths and Centaurs were identical. Hyginus 33 is a very confused account of Hercules, Deianira, Centaurs and Lapiths, which may have misled Joseph, but it must be admitted that the reference in Ovid at *Met*.9.191 is unambiguously to Centaurs.

124. apples: these were the golden apples to be obtained from the garden of the Hesperides. They were guarded by a dragon that had to be killed by Hercules before gaining access to the apples.

Antaeus: see 1.285n. Joseph has added a further ingenious touch here. According to Vat.Myth.3.13.4 Hercules was an astronomer, so his skill in teaching Antaeus, who was a geometrician (as a son of Mother Earth, Ge) about the stars refers both tc his intellectual and wrestling abilities.

126f. Achelous was one of the suitors for Deianira defeated in combat by Hercules. When Hercules was returning home with her he carelessly entrusted her to Nessus, a Centaur, while he crossed a deep river. Nessus attempted to abscond with her but was killed by Hercules' poisoned arrow. Cf. Vat.Myth.1.58 and 2.165, Ovid, *Met*.9.1-133.

128. horses of Diomedes: both Ovid (*Met*.9.194) and Hyginus (30) say that Hercules killed the horses, while other sources say he killed Diomedes but took the horses back to Eurystheus.

129. Hippolyte: Queen of the Amazons tamed by Hercules. He then gave her girdle to Eurystheus and Hippolyte herself to Theseus as a wife. The glossators, presumably interpreting the taking of her girdle as a euphemism for rape, suggest that Hercules taught her to prefer sex to fighting. Cf. Hyginus 30.

Stymphalians: the glossators think that these were a people named after a river, but it is unlikely that Joseph made this mistake. Hyginus (20 and 30) calls them birds while Vat.Myth.1 and 3 equate them with the Harpies. The reference in Ovid (*Met*.9.187) is very vague and may be behind the error of the glossators.

130. The earth owes Hercules a debt of gratitude because of all the monsters he killed; the heavens because he held them

on his shoulders to give Atlas a rest.

131. you were a carrier: see previous note.
you will be carried: refers to 135 where his new bride, Hebe, will 'carry' him in the marriage bed. *Vector* is the correct reading in both cases. As the glossators point out, it is one of a group of nouns that are both active and passive. *Alumnus* and *hospes* are cited. Cf. *Grecismus* p.71, 314-15.

133. si iusseris, ibunt: cf. Juv.3.78.

134. monstra: Hercules would be ideally suited to remove these.

135. Juno: she is now on Hercules' side, after having been the cause of all his labours on earth. It is not easy to say why she changed her feelings toward him to the extent of giving him her daughter Hebe for a wife.

141. videri: historic infinitive.

142. queri: historic infinitive.

143. captiva: I take this in its classical meaning rather than its medieval meaning 'wretched'. Cf. Eng. 'caitiff', Fr. *chétif*, and Hugh Primas, 6.11.

145-49. Joseph has expanded Virgil's description of the 'wedding' of Dido and Aeneas in *Aen*.4.160ff.

150. enemy: Ajax. See 1.348n.

152. cimbia: Joseph is continuing the incongruous nature of the wedding feast as these are sacrificial vessels.

153. Cf. Ovid, *Her*.11.54.

155. Trojan: Antenor.

161f. minus uno..gradu: a very involved way of saying that Telamon was the grandson of Jupiter. He was the son of Aeacus, son of Jupiter.

165. The hardships suffered on land and sea have been borrowed from the opening of the *Aeneid*, and the inappropriateness of the use of the phrase by Antenor is further evidence of his villainy.

172. brides: Joseph uses *faces* 'torches' (used in wedding ceremonies) for the brides themselves!

175. rapienda minatur: another bold construction: *rapienda* is used for *se raptum iri* and she is not really the one who is threatening. This speech, like that of Priam, is very formal and rhetorical.

176f. Note the involved, unnatural way Joseph makes Antenor speak here. Alcides is not strictly a patronymic as Alcaeus was Hercules' putative grandfather, while calling Pollux 'a mistake' (*error*), because he was an identical twin of Castor and thus liable to be mistaken for him, is very artificial.

Noverat..novit seems to suggest that Joseph is making some distinction here, but the import escapes me.

178ff. Antenor insists on the worthlessness of Hesione: the other Greeks were only too ready to give her to Telamon amongst the trivia; if Priam had any other relative left he would not have bothered about Hesione. Antenor's use of *trusisset* further suggests that he did not think the journey was worth the effort and signals to the Greeks that his views differ from those of his king, thus preparing the way for his treachery in Book 6, and giving Paris some cause for his doubts about Antenor's handling of the embassy (191-92). By calling Priam *infelix* however, Antenor reverts to a correct style of pleading by using *captatio benevolentiae*, but then subverts the mission by making no effort to convey the humility of Priam's letter.

186. Telamon's claim to have earned the right to Hesione's love through his sword is not correct. He was a sapper in the attack on Troy. The sentiment seems closer to that of a medieval knight who earns the affections of his lady by his prowess in a tournament or in battle when the ladies watched from the battlements. Hesione obviously did not feel any admiration for him.

187. Dirceum: a fountain near Thebes. The quotation is from Stat.*Theb*.2.429. Cf. also Albert of Stade, *Troilus* 1.213.

188. Dares 5 *ad fin*.

191. unjust: Paris' suspicions are unjust because he has misinterpreted the reasons behind the failure of Antenor's embassy. He thinks Antenor came to a secret agreement with the Greeks whereas the failure was due to Antenor's lack of professionalism. The argument between them reflects the differences between the Trojan royal family and the rest of the Trojans which Dictys used to such effect.

193. sibi commodus uni: Cf. Hor. *Ep*.1.9.9.

198. Hector's objections, of which this is Joseph's only mention, are set out in full in a speech in Dares, in which Hector declared himself ready to invade Greece but convinced that the invasion would fail because of Europe's warlike qualities and the inexperience of Trojans in building ships. Joseph is not particularly interested in the narrative aspects of the epic, and in keeping with medieval practice he does not cover extensively what his source gives in full.

199. Although the Syrtes were strictly sandbanks off the Libyan coast, they are used to denote the dangers of the sea.

200. heavenly power: Venus.
203. The dream of Paris: Paris' judging of the beauty contest is rationalised by Dares (7), who interprets the event as a dream. Whereas he spends little time on it, Joseph makes it a tour de force of forensic oratory, drawing on all his rhetorical skills and knowledge of mythology. The goddesses become progressively more prolix, innuendoes are rife. Joseph seems to revel in the depiction of these bitchy females like most of the Latin writers of his time, possibly because of his ecclesiastical education, possibly as a reaction to the growing importance of French vernacular literature which emphasised the role and influence of women. However, Joseph's portrayal of the women is far more subtle than that achieved by his fellow Latin writers with the possible exception of Walter Map, whose characterisation of the queen in his *Sadius and Galo* rivals most of the vernacular creations. This story of a male presiding over a female beauty contest is probably Joseph's rejoinder to the stories of the courts of love, where Henry II's wife Eleanor of Aquitaine and her daughters presided over 'courts' in which men's failings as lovers were judged.
203. Aurora: her parents are normally given as Hyperion and Thea or possibly Titan and Terra. Joseph typically uses the least well-known version, that her father was Pallas, brother of Perseus, which he found in Ovid, *Met*.9.421 and 15.191 and 700.
205. cold tears: the dew.
208ff. This method of separating three sentences into their grammatical components was a common poetic technique taught in the schools. Cf. 3.253-54 and Faral (1962^2) 361 n.1.
211. Paris insists on the divine intervention. He did not just lose his way.
213. goddesses: Juno, Pallas, Venus.
218. Cirream..iuventam: Cirrha was a town at the foot of Mt Parnassus where Apollo was worshipped (Lucan 3.172); *iuventam* indicates youth or greenness. The two together give an evergreen tree sacred to Apollo, i.e. the laurel.
222. gratissimus error: Hor. *Ep*.2.2.140 and Virg.*Aen*.10.392.
232. sleep of the sort..: the source for this interpretation of sleep comes from Macrobius *in Somnium Scipionis* 1.3.15.
235. greatest: Juno.
239. my beloved stepson: Mercury. He was the only child of Jupiter's many extra-marital affairs that Juno raised at her breast.

241. only love: Joseph seems intent on undermining the goddess' credibility. Cf. also 245.

250. Pallas..Medusa: see 2.24n. Juno's polite start now turns into a sustained attack on her fellow contestants. The insults begin with Pallas being maligned as goddess of war.

254f. dira..diva: this example of paronomasia I have been unable to translate satisfactorily into English. Glossator P points out that this often happens in the vernacular, quoting as an example 'singe mes sire' (monkey sir). Unfortunately he does not give the correct form. Glossator A glosses similarly but omits the French which would have been incomprehensible for an Austrian reader.

256ff. snakes..horned serpents: these are presumably those associated with the Gorgon's head, but Juno is probably lying in suggesting that Pallas did not have normal hair.

264. learned Minerva: Juno now refers to her as goddess of wisdom.

266. Juno unjustly suggests that Jupiter was not Pallas' father, and then attempts further character assassination by asking (and thus contradicting herself) which whore was her mother. The use of 'our' is very demeaning. In fact it is difficult to know whether Juno is deliberately throwing any insult at Pallas or is referring to the version of the legend that made Metis her mother. The normal version is that she was born fully-grown from Jupiter's brain without any sexual intercourse being involved in her conception. Juno refers to this immediately afterwards.

269. keeps only man in mind: all Pallas' pursuits are virile. In fact this is not true either, as spinning, weaving and embroidery are also associated with her. *virago = vir ago* 'act as a man'.

271f. Mavortia..mares vorat: as with *dira/diva* it has proved difficult to reproduce in English the effect of the Latin. This type of definition by 'etymology', quite common in 12th-c. literature, is based on an ancient practice, but whereas a writer like Giraldus Cambrensis has a much more sensible approach to language and etymology, in the present context of a dispute between women it is hard to discover what Joseph's own views were. The practice of taking syllables from different words is obviously quite arbitrary as in *mares vorat*. In fact *Mavortia* is based on the ancient form of *Mars - Mavors*.

272f. Pallas: 'pallid' is a 'reasonable' interpretation by Juno here, but 'because she slit Pallas' throat' is ludicrous.

Glossator P thinks the dead Pallas was the giant killed in the attack on heaven, while A prefers to think of Evander's son who was killed by Turnus when he was under the influence of the goddess of war. He does retain the possibility of the Pallas in question being the giant.

275. Juno now addresses Venus.

283f. heres..heres: *traductio* cf. Faral (1962[2]) 322.

284f. Cf. Ovid, *Met*.2.368-69.

285f. one chosen from a number: again Juno contradicts what she has just said.

288. pari parit: again paronomasia. Through the words of Mother Nature Juno has now mentioned two features of a good wife, namely beauty and fecundity. She now adds the third component, chastity, when she points out that she was an unwilling partner to her brother's lust.

289. Cf. Avianus 35.13.

291. Ericina: this term for Venus derives from the temple dedicated to her worship on Mt Eryx in Sicily. Juno believes that the fact that she was chosen as Jupiter's wife proves that she is more beautiful.

293. Paphos: a city on Cyprus famous for the worship of Venus. pure birth: Juno is using heavy irony as the next line shows.

294. testicles: of her father, Saturn.

295. Jupiter a father: Jupiter attempted to seduce and even to rape her but she resisted successfully. Among her children were Harmonia, Cupid and Anteros, fathered by Mars.

296. human race: this sarcasm is directed towards her affairs with humans, e.g. as mother of Aeneas by Anchises.

298. A reference to the famous story of Vulcan catching his wife Venus in bed with Mars and covering them with his net while Apollo (the sun) shone to indicate their whereabouts.

300f. The pun on *Lennius (Lemnius)* and *lenius* is impossible to reproduce in English.

302. the Phrygian: Anchises.

303f. The 'etymologies' are again mixed here: *alma = alit malum*.

305. There was a time: this refers to the story of Tiresias, named at 308. He was called upon by Jupiter and Juno to put an end to their argument on which sex derived the more pleasure from the sexual act. Presumably Venus was called upon in her capacity as goddess of love, Pallas as goddess of wisdom.

309. But I will say no more: a veiled warning to Paris who would have been aware of the punishment Juno meted on Tiresias

for not judging her the winner.
Trojan: Paris.

310. Joseph has toned down the blatant bribery evident in most accounts, e.g. *Excidium Troie*, but still has Juno conveying to Paris the notions of power and gold if he names her as winner.
313. In her summing up Juno reverts to her main positive argument, her relationship with Jupiter, but this time in the form of a warning, making her strongest point in her final line.
320. sacred: because she is the goddess of wisdom.
322. famous Trojan: it was because Paris was famous that he was chosen by Jupiter to act as judge. It is also *captatio benevolentiae*.
323. whatever merit: this sign of humility is in stark contrast to Juno's attitude and tone.
325. Joseph ingeniously incorporates his anti-feminism in the words of a woman without sacrificing credibility.
329. honour: ironic. Pallas cleverly praises Juno's speech only to dismiss it as irrelevant.

333ff. *Captatio benevolentiae*, pointing out her own inferior status.

336ff. Note the sound rhetorical technique of using triple structures.

342. wreck any marriage: this is aimed at Venus.
catch my husband doing wrong: Juno is the target.
343. She reveals that all her pursuits are not manly in her words to Paris because he has sisters, and she wishes to ingratiate herself with him.
350. It is typical of the virile Pallas that she should use *viribus* 'strengths' for *virtutibus* 'virtues'.
352. regnum mobile: the sea. The reference is to Jupiter's destruction of the world in the time of Deucalion and Pyrrha (Ovid, *Met.*1) which brought about the need for a Pallas to guide the virtues of mankind. Cf. 362 and 370.
361. vindice: the glossators point out that this is an incorrect usage, as *vindex* is strictly a defender, but this is not certain.

365f. Pallas prefers the version of being conceived without any sex being involved, thus refuting Juno's remarks at 266.

367. more pleasing: because wisdom was born.
373. we all know the story: *occupatio*. Cf. Faral (1962[2]) 233, Lawler 124.

373ff. Phlegra etc: refers to the battle of the Titans against heaven. Vat.Myth.2.53 mentions Enceladus, Briareus and Typhoeus but gives no details. Cf. Ovid, *Met*.5.315-31.

374. Cyclops: they had to make so many thunderbolts for Jupiter to throw at the Titans that they were exhausted.

375. Briareus: a hundred-handed giant. Joseph talks of the hundred quivers and of the arrows of Niobe when referring to the hundred arrows of Apollo and Diana (metonymy) and the arrows that killed Niobe and her children.

378. warlike Juno: returning Juno's similar insult at 271.

379f. Presumably these details of a sexual nature are Joseph's own invention. They are not entirely gratuitous, however, as they will provide Venus with material to impugn Pallas' modesty.

383f. Medusa the Gorgon goddess: answering Juno's remarks at 251.

384. gold of my armour: see 261.

387. nostrum est quod regnat: Cf. Persius 5.151.

389. heavenly one: see 255.
virago: see 269.

391. Pallas overcomes her modesty in order to show her breasts to Paris. Cf. 3.237 where Helen would have liked to do the same but was stopped by her sense of decency!

392f. See Juno's remarks at 259.

393. horned serpents: see 258.

395. Vulcan: Pallas now turns Juno's attack on Venus (298-301) to her own advantage, pointing out that Vulcan is Juno's son and that he is neither warlike nor a weaver of the right sort of material. Note the irony in 'powerful' which she then deflates with *molli*. In case her point is missed she glances at Venus.

400. etymologises: presumably referring to *Mavortia* from *mares vorat*.
derivation: from *palleo* or *Pallas*.

401. more irony.

402. mollius equo: this picks up Juno's insult to Venus (*mollior equo* 276) but alters the meaning.

403. polleo: 'to be powerful'. Again this play on words is untranslatable.

404. Pallas is losing the humble attitude she adopted at the start of her speech, but as at 322 and 343 is keeping her judge in a favourable frame of mind by addressing him in flattering fashion whereas Juno had addressed him with '*tu, Fryx*' (309).

406. offended the gods: by outshining them in the battle against the giants.

407. Juno's example: see 288-89.
408. unworthy: referring to the various lies Juno told. Pallas contrasts her own truthful statements (309), but see 422n.
409. sed taceo: picks up Juno's remark at 309 but without any threat to Paris.
411f. she now turns her attention to Venus, the Cyprian (415).
413. Note the alliteration and paronomasia.
416. golden axe: a reference to the story of Mercury who found a peasant crying on a river bank because he had dropped his axe in the water. Mercury fished a golden axe out of the river but the peasant said it was not his. To reward him Mercury gave him the axe he had lost together with the golden one. See Hor. *Sat*.1.7.27. Joseph therefore uses 'golden axe' for 'reward for honesty'.
418f. Note the oxymoron in these lines.
419f. Note the alliteration.
422. Vulcan: in fact there is no record of Venus having any children by Vulcan, so Joseph must be putting lies into Pallas' mouth.
428. Bacchus' other name was *'Liber'* (= free). Again the wordplay is untranslatable.
the sea: Aegeon is a sea-god (Ovid, *Met*.2.10), here used for the sea itself.
429. late avenger: Pallas sees Venus' troubling of the gods as a form of late revenge for the deposition of her father, Saturn.
430. cold father: Saturn was considered to be a cold planet.
pen..: this form of aposiopesis can be parallelled in other 12th-c. works (e.g. *tu au(tem)* in *Ysengrimus* 1.98) yet does not appear in the teaching manuals.
431. noble, all-powerful: ironic. *Strenuus* would be apposite when describing a knight.
435ff. These lines are proleptic, referring to the siege of Troy.
438. cedes cedit: paronomasia.
441ff. prey: this again seems proleptic, referring to the person of Helen as prey, causing the destruction of Troy. Thus the Trojans get some consolation from the Greeks' loss of Helen while the Greeks get some from the destruction of Troy.
444. Protheus: a sea-god who could change his shape at will (see Ovid, *Met*.2.9 and 8.731; Virg. *Geo*.4.425). Pallas is saying that just as it is impossible to force Proteus so it is impossible to recount all Venus' changes.

449. greatest: more use of flattery.

450. Pallas refers again (cf. 343) to her various skills to ingratiate herself with Paris: Mars because Paris and some of his brothers were warriors; Clio because, as one of the Muses, she presided over wisdom, influencing Helenus and Cassandra; Arachne because of his sisters and their weaving. Pallas' choice of Arachne probably carries the hint of a warning to Paris as Arachne was punished by Pallas for her contemptuous attitude.

454. fate of Troy: Pallas finishes on a clearer warning. She reminds Paris that the fate of Troy depends on her.

459. Venus is the third to speak. Her speech shows a much cleverer use of rhetoric than those of the other goddesses. Whereas Juno had based her claim to the title on her authority as Queen of Heaven and wife of Jupiter, and Pallas on her abilities in war, wisdom, weaving and virginity, Venus starts by speaking humbly and then identifying herself with mankind before going on to demolish the arguments of the other two. At the end she reveals all her beauty, proof that she fully understood what the 'case' was all about.

462. good: Joseph may mean 'second' (heaven being the first), or he may have both meanings in mind.

463. Only the gods are jealous of her.

473. Her address to Paris is much more human and warm.
refute or blame: In fact she will go on to do just that, but first she praises her rivals for their competence, suggesting at the same time her own inferiority.

480. aggressive plain-speaking: referring to Pallas' appearance and tone in speaking the truth. See 405 and 410.

482. Tritonian: Pallas was often called this because of her worship near Lake Tritonis in Africa. Cf. Virg.*Aen*.2.171 and Ovid, *Met*.2.783 and 794.

483. greatest of the Muses: Venus intelligently leaves aside the defamation of character based on etymology and touches on the question of Pallas' truthfulness.

488. Phillidas, Ysiphilas: See Persius 1.34 for the joining of these two names. Phyllis was loved by Demophoon, son of Theseus, but committed suicide when she thought she had been deserted by him. Joseph could have known the story from Ovid (*Her*.2, *Ars Am*.2.353, *Tr*.2.437), Hyginus 59, Vat.Myth.1.159 or 2.214. Hypsipyle, Queen of Lemnos, was loved and deserted by Jason. Joseph is being both ingenious and ingenuous here. Presumably Venus assumed

that these stories were being referred to by Pallas, but it is not clear where. Perhaps the reference is to 445, but if so, it is so allusive that only Joseph/Venus recognised it. While the allusiveness of Pallas' speech is obviously contrasted with the plainness of Venus', Joseph's condemnation of it is ambivalent when one considers that he is an expert exponent of the art of allusion.

490f. Note the alliteration.

492. who, what and why: a medieval touch. In their *Accessus ad Auctores*, or introductions to authors, teachers used the 'who, what, why' method. Cf. *Alexandreis* 1.531.

493. gelide: while it is tempting to take this as a genitive singular accompanying *virginis* ('cold virgin') by which Venus would be returning the insult that Pallas cast on her father (430), glossator A defines it as an adverb going with *fando*. *Nec..gelide nil improba fando* is then 'speaking mendaciously some shameful things'.

495ff. Venus uses the rhetorical device of *contrapositio*, very common in medieval writers.

500. Anchises: referring to 302 (Juno's speech).

502. your Aeneas: *captatio benevolentiae*.

503. ruin: referring back to 420.

505. popular: see 345.

506. men she destroys in war: a clever allusion to Juno's attempt at etymology (271-72) which endorses the thought without accepting the wording.

508. sluggish and cowardly: see 388.

510. Aglauros..serpent: reference to the story of Vulcan who attempted to rape Pallas and unsuccessfully ejaculated his semen on to her thigh. Pallas collected the semen from which Erichthonius was born. He had serpents' tails for legs (cf. Vat.Myth.2.37). Pallas shut him up in a basket which she gave to the daughters of Cecrops for safe keeping with instructions not to open it. However, one of the daughters, Aglauros, did open it and so she guessed Pallas' secret. Ovid, *Met*.2.562 speaks of a child and a serpent.

511. sed taceo: Venus echoes Pallas' echo (409) of Juno (309) to refute Pallas' claim to virginity.
facie pollet: note how Joseph again picks up an etymology - this time the 'correct' one given by Pallas - only to modify it. See 506n.

512. reflection of the swollen cheeks: Venus is just as allusive as Pallas. The reference here is to the story of Pallas playing

a flute and seeing her reflection in the water. When she saw her puffed-out cheeks she was horrified at her ugliness and threw away the flute. Venus thus destroys Pallas' claim to beauty. Cf. Hyginus 165; Vat.Myth.1.125.

513. assumed: good fighting is a virile quality. As a woman Pallas had borrowed or assumed it and so could not claim it as her own.

516. power-struggle of the gods: this refers back to Pallas' claim at 373-89. Venus here suggests that another version of the legend is nearer the truth. Cf. 113n. Hyginus 60 might well be in Joseph's mind here.

519. cowardly Olympus: refers back to Pallas' claim at 388 and her sarcastic echo (383-84) of Juno's insult (251). Venus' remark ironically mentions Pallas as a shade or shadow while *extorsit* suggests that the *titulos palmamque* were not really hers.

520. believe it: Venus is destroying Pallas' credibility without disproving it.

521f. The irony is heavy.

523. mine: Joseph cannot resist an attack on women, even when he is trying to make this woman a sympathetic figure.
grandchildren: Venus now turns her attention to Juno. The grandchildren in question are Cupid, Anteros and Harmonia, all fathered on Venus by Mars, son of Jupiter.

524. not too presumptuous: note the mock humility of Venus.

525. socium..genus: for *sociam generis*.

526. defenders: i.e. Juno and Pallas.

527. mother of snakes: Harmonia along with her husband Cadmus were changed into snakes when they were weary of life, having seen their children persecuted by Juno.

528. exile: Cadmus, whose father Agenor had sent him away from home in search of his sister Europa.

529. populum: Joseph is exaggerating somewhat the number of Harmonia and Cadmus' children. There were only five!

533. Semele: one of the daughters of Harmonia and Cadmus. She was made pregnant by Jupiter and would have given birth to Bacchus had she survived Juno's hostility. Bacchus was said to have been saved by Jupiter from Semele's womb and kept by him in his thigh until birth.

535. Juno appeared to Semele disguised as Beroe (548), an old woman, and persuaded Semele to ask Jupiter to come to her bed with the same majesty as he approached Juno. Jupiter swore (iurato 537) to do so and this resulted in Semele's death. The portrait of Beroe was a standard feature in

medieval literature. Joseph was too good a poet to include one in his epic. Cf. Faral (1962[2]) 130-32.

538. year-long journey: The source of this information is unknown to me. Venus started the whole account at 527, talking of Cadmus' exile while looking for Europa, then went on to his marriage with Harmonia, followed by the disasters to their children, particularly Semele, before returning to the story of Europa. Venus next uses the Europa story as an attack on Juno's lack of sex-appeal and beauty.

554. stabilique thoro: this looks like a sarcastic remark made with the *Aeneid* in mind. Juno is of course the goddess of marriage who offered a stable marriage to Aeolus (Aen.1.73) and later for Dido (4.126), each time using the adjective *stabilis* and each time unsuccessfully.

555f. Joseph is offering a justification for a husband's infidelity which would please his fellow men. The source for this is *Proverbs* 21.19.

560. golden: the Golden Age was said to have occurred under Saturn's rule.

561. daughter: Venus now uses her lineage to bolster her claim just as the other two goddesses had done.

563. equal of Minerva: Venus now suggests that she is not inferior to Pallas and she plays on Paris' feelings by recalling her status as an exile. It was, in fact, Juno who said she had no equal. See 280.

569ff. Venus now associates herself with other sea-goddesses in general and with Thetis in particular who could be greater than Juno, thus making herself greater than Juno by implication. For the story of Thetis cf. 1.342n. She obliquely answers (570-71) the accusation of Juno (293-94) and Pallas (428-30) about her less-than-decent birth.

571. vindex: this time used correctly. Cf. 361n.

575. whore: Venus turns Juno's insult against Pallas (266) against Juno and at the same time negates Juno's claim to be the bride of Jupiter (238).

578. gold: reference to Juno's offer at 310.

579. An allusion to an etymological or derivation-type explanation of the name of Paris, based on *par* 'equal' according to certain writers. His reputation for fairness came from his crowning of Mars who, in the form of a bull, had defeated Paris' favourite bull in a fight. The fullest versions of this story are found in *Excidium Troie* p.4 and Hyginus 91. Ovid, *Her*.15.360 refers to the origin of the name.

582. she: Juno. It was because Juno stirred up Hercules that Hesione was abducted and so many Trojans were killed.
585. battle-prowess: refers to Pallas' claims at 327 and 372-89.
586. Fate: the statue of Pallas which should have protected Troy. Cf. 1.544 and 2.454.
abducted Trojan: Ganymedes who replaced Juno in Jupiter's bed - an oblique allusion to Pallas' remark about Juno being kicked out of bed by Persephone (383). Jupiter made Ganymedes cup-bearer to the gods in place of Juno's daughter, Hebe. Joseph probably has Juv.5.60-61 in mind here, but the association of Ganymedes and the Judgement of Paris recalls Juno's complaint at Virg.*Aen* 1.27-28.
587. molliter: only in Venus' mouth does *mollis* or *molliter* have a meaning that is not pejorative. Cf. Juno's *mollior equo* (276), Pallas' *pede molli* (396) and *molles* (440).
589. of gods: all the Trojans were said to be descended from Dardanus, son of Jupiter.
flos Asie: Juv.5.56.
590. unstable verses: i.e. elegiac couplets.
591. frightened girls: together with the last reference this picks up Pallas' claims at 343-44 and 450.
592. Phoebus: a very cryptic allusion to Marsyas who did compete with Phoebus when Pallas had thrown away her flute. Cf. 512n. and Hyginus 165.
Arachne: see 450n.
596. greater than half the world: it was common in the Middle Ages to think of Asia as being greater than the combined size of the other two known continents, Europe and Africa.
600. gift: Helen.
605f. Venus refers to herself as Vesperus, the evening star that appears after the setting of the sun, and as Lucifer, the morning star that appears before sunrise. Cf. *Grecismus* p.72. 339-40.
607. tears off her cloak: Joseph is again using the *Excidium Troie* in which Venus does just this to appear completely naked to Paris (p.5).
608. humeros: as glossator A points out, this is synechdoche, using the part for the whole.
609. Joseph does not need to describe the handing over of the prize. He merely notes the effect of Venus' victory on Juno and Pallas.
610. Having finished recounting his dream Paris now encourages the Trojans.
611f. sompnia..pondus habent: Cf. Ovid, *Met*.9.495.

BOOK THREE

1. silence of the deliberations: one must assume that Paris had consulted the council of elders about his proposed foray to Greece. The expression *consulta silentia* is very bold and typical of Joseph, particularly in this opening passage.
2. Ydalium Peana: although a paean was literally a song of praise to Apollo, the addition of a qualifying adjective made its use more general. Thus one finds e.g. Herculeum Peana, or as here, *Ydalium*, designating Venus. In support of this usage the glossators cite Claudian 2.11 *omnis Io paean regio sonat*.
3. una..una: *traductio*. The first *una* is adjectival, the second adverbial. *una Venus = nomen Veneris solum*. Cf. Lawler 20.
4. altus: past participle of *alo* 'I feed'. Joseph applies it to *sanguis* which he uses to mean *hostia* 'victim'.
5. i.e. there are no oxen left to plough the fields as they are all being sacrificed!
7. Inachis: Io, the daughter of Inachus, was changed into a cow. A possible source is Ovid, *Fasti* 1.454, where Inachis is used as a patronymic for Io.
10. An ingenious variation on Virg.*Geo*.2.139.
11ff. In these carefully constructed half-line units Joseph puts forward the superiority of the Christian God over the pagan gods, using Ovid, *Ex Ponto* 4.8.39ff as his inspiration.
18. honey etc: I have not attempted to translate these Statian-like circumlocutions literally as Joseph is being particularly recondite. *Aristeos latices*: Aristaeus was famous as a beekeeper (Virg.*Geo*.4 or Ovid, *Ex Ponto* 4.2.9). *Melibea fluenta*: Meliboeus is a shepherd in Virgil's *Eclogues*.
19. Ycareos haustus: Icarius was an Athenian whom Bacchus used to spread the drinking of wine. Hyginus 130 is the likely source for this, though a commentary on Ovid, *Met*.6.125 might have yielded the information. In Vat.Myth.2.61 and 3.15.6 he is called Icarus.
    fracti Phenicis odores: when the Phoenix was aged (*fractus*), after several thousand centuries of life, it committed suicide on a funeral pyre of herbs. The cinders were considered to be highly aromatic.
23. Ydaliam delibat avem: this is probably the only real problem in the establishment of the text. Sedgwick (1930), 55, found it problematic because it seemed to indicate the

slaughter of a dove when Priam's sacrifice is obviously bloodless. He raised the question of the possibility of some other meaning but Gompf did not entertain this idea, preferring to emend to *Ybleam..opem*, citing 46 in support. While this is an attractive emendation Gompf offers no explanation for the fact that all the MSS and the two glossators read *Ydaliam..avem*, nor how the error would have arisen with the intervening verb being retained. I have preferred to retain the MS reading and follow Sedgwick's line of thought, giving the verb its meaning at 231 'touch lightly'. The Idalian bird is the dove sacred to Venus.

25. our Tritonian Neptune: Neptune had helped in the original construction of Troy.
26. Thetios: see 1.79n.
37. husband-to-be: Paris.
38. solatam solare: note the paronomasia.
39. Inachias: a name given to the Greeks from the Argive king, Inachus. See 7. The thought, however, contradicts 37.
41. abduction: of Hesione, presumably. Cf. 2.168-69 where Antenor says that Juno will not approve of the marriage of Hesione and Telamon.
44. the old order: Joseph uses the image of the old die being upturned, but if he has some passage in mind I am unaware of it. Sedgwick (1930), 61, sees *alea* as representing *Fortuna*.
45. Eneadas: by using this patronymic to denote the Trojans Priam is appealing to Venus. They would not be thus called until after the destruction of Troy.
46. Hyblaean honey: Mt Hybla in Sicily was famous for its honey.
47. nidor: the glossators take Joseph to task, pointing out that this word should be used only for the smell of roast meat.
49. another sort of heat: Helenus breaks out into a sweat when prophesying.
51. vocales usus: for *usus vocis*.
57. Deiphobus: the reference may possibly be to the story in Hyginus 91 where he wanted to kill Paris. If he had done so Troy would not have fallen.
70. Alexander: this was his name before acquiring that of Paris when his impartiality became famous.
Sybil of Cumae: famous from Virg.*Aen*.6. She was old because she forgot to ask for eternal youth when Apollo

granted her to live as many years as she had grains of sand in her hand.

71. ram of Libya: in Libya was found the oracle of Jupiter Ammon. A likely source for this information is Lucan 9. Cf.1.549.
birds of Chaonia: Jupiter made oracular statements in Chaonia through the medium of brass doves in oak trees. Cf. Lucan 6.426, Claudian, *De Raptu Pros*. 3.47 and Virg.*Aen*.3.335.

74. plebes: antique form of *plebs*. The passage is a further revelation of Joseph's dislike of the lower classes.

86. grim feasts: reference to the story of Atreus and Thyestes. Atreus fed bits of Thyestes' sons to him in revenge for Thyestes' adultery with his wife. Glossator P confuses the two brothers while for once giving a more detailed version of events.

91. Tirynthian hero: Hercules.
Nessum: for *vestem Nessi*. For a similar construction cf.5.242 *indutus Achillem*. This alludes to the continuation of the story adumbrated at 2.127. On dying, Nessus dipped his shirt in his blood and gave it to Deianira to use as a love charm should Hercules' love for her diminish. As the arrow that killed him was poisoned, the poison impregnated the shirt.

93. our nationality: this recalls Venus' comment at 2.597.

101. Euphorbius: Euphorbus is the correct name. The relationship between these two is reversed by Joseph, following Dares 8. In Ovid, *Met*.15.161 Euphorbus is the son of Panthus. It might have been possible to interpret *Euforbius* as an adjective 'the Euphorbian father' were it not for the fact that at 102 we have *proles* 'son' and the prophecy is definitely by Panthus. Euphorbus (sic) is found again at 5.412 where he is killed by Achilles, again contrary to the Ovidian evidence which gives Menelaus as the slayer of Euphorbus. Euphorbus is not elsewhere associated with prophecy whereas Panthus is said to have learnt his prophetic skill from his father Othryas, priest of Apollo. All the MSS agree on the readings *Euforbius* (101) and *proles* (102).

103. Helene: this is a variant nominative to the more usual Helena. Cf. also 223 and 330.

105. the new: another complaint about the modern and the old. Cf.1.15n.

108. audit et audet: paronomasia. Cf. Albert of Stade 1.483.

110. Dares 8.
116. Trojan girl: Hesione.
118f. Adynata.
121f. story: referring to 2.188-91.
136. Antenor again incites the Trojans to war. Cf. 2.191.
145. shirt of fire: cf. 91n. Again Joseph uses a bold expression, *ignes*, for *vestem venenatam*.
146. two sons of Aeacus: Peleus and Telamon.
147. boy or girl: a reference to the stay of Achilles in Lycomedes' harem disguised as a girl to avoid being called up to join the Greek army. His mother, Thetis, had put him there on hearing an oracle say that her son would either die young in war or live long in peace.
151. prophetic opponents: e.g. Helenus. The meaning seems to be that they will return from Greece as victors, but instead of holding a triumphal procession they will hand over their swords to doubters such as Helenus and Hector (cf. 2.198n.) who are regarded as enemies (*hostibus*).
155. shepherd: see 2.579n. The following lines allude to further details of the story. When Hecuba was expecting Paris she dreamed she was giving birth to a flaming torch. This was interpreted as an omen foretelling that the child would be the cause of the destruction of Troy. Although Hecuba was told to kill the child she exposed it on the mountain where it was found by a shepherd. Thus Paris was brought up as a shepherd. When he was a young man he went to Troy, competed in the games, and defeated Hector, Deiphobus and others. It was only the revelation of his true identity that saved his life.
158. Cisseida: Hecuba was the daughter of Cisseus.
162. Dares 9.
163. pinnacles: these would denote warships.
large fleet: Paris is supposed to have set sail with twenty-two ships which Aeneas would later use for his escape from Troy. His own ship (*pinus*) was taken from Mt Ida where the castrated priests of Cybele, the Galli, worshipped in a frenzied manner. Joseph is probably using wordplay again, *pinus* (penis) - *ementulati*. They castrated themselves in imitation of Attis, Cybele's lover driven mad by her. Attis was changed into a pine-tree. Cf. Ovid, *Met*.10.104ff. and *Fasti* 4.223ff., Vat.Myth.1.230 and 3.2. Note the Lucan-style use of negatives in this passage, e.g. *non induit..non adversante*.
166. Cibebe: all MSS give Cibele which is unmetrical. At 1.539

and 6.585 Cibele is correctly scanned. One solution might be to write *Cibelle* (cf. *relligio* 3.153), but *Cibebe* is the form found in both passages from the Vatican Mythographers adduced in the previous note.

168-73. The description of the ship shows how much progress had been made in shipbuilding since the launching of the Argo at 1.78-90.

171. Tiro: Tyrian purple.
Tago: gold from the River Tagus.
Indus: ivory from India.

178. ferri: with *fremere* and *miscere* (180) historic infinitives.

181. Nabatheos: here Phrygians, though poets like Ovid, Lucan and Juvenal often use the name to denote any eastern people. Strictly speaking the Arabians should be thus designated. Glossator A quotes Ovid, *Met*.1.61.

184. Paeonians: these were a people of Macedonia thought to have once been Trojans. Joseph's most likely source of information is a commentary on Ovid, *Met*.5, where the name occurs at 303 and 313.

185. Aeneas' role as traitor is not overstressed by Joseph. His trip to Greece with Paris helped him to make contact with the Greeks before the war while the arrogance of the Trojan royal family alienated him from the Trojan cause during it. Joseph refers to his presence here with Polydamas, and in Book 6 they liaise secretly with the Greeks.

188. Cassandra: another of Priam's children who had the gift of prophecy through Apollo, but she was destined never to be believed. Her brother Helenus was often listened to, though not on this occasion (cf.154). This, like the allusive reference at 6.461, seems to indicate that Joseph is aware of, and acknowledging, the legend that made Helenus virtually a traitor.

192. Cf. Ovid, *Her*.6.65.

193. Cf. Lucan 4.735.

195. content with Hesione: this repeats the words at 40 but does little to resolve the question of Priam's real feelings.

198. Cithera: I have translated this as Cerigo, the island off the Greek coast, but the plural verb *patuere* shows that Joseph is using it as a plural. The glossators seem somewhat at a loss, commenting lamely '*loca quedam sunt in Grecia*'. At 211 Joseph plainly calls it an island.

200. Simoontide: an adjective formed from the river Simois in Troy. For the event cf. Dares 9.

201. qui, quo, unde: cf. 2.492n.
205. Hermione: daughter of Helen and Menelaus.
206. matrem secundam: based on the view that *matertera* 'maternal aunt' is a shortened form of *mater altera*. Clytemnestra is the person in question here.
212. myrtle-bearing goddess: Venus.
213. falcatur in arcus: cf. Ovid, *Met*.11.229 and *Her*.2.131.
218. Rumour: cf. Virg.*Aen*.4.173.
222. Helea: Dares is the source for this information.
235. self-control: this favourable view of Helen is quickly undermined by 237.
240. ardet et audet: paronomasia. cf. 108.
246. Dares 10.
251. Cicero: cf. Faral (1962[2]) 92. In the medieval comedy *Miles Gloriosus* we find (82) *Nummus ubi loquitur Tullius ipse silet*.
253f. As glossator P advises, 'redde singula singulis'. For the separation of noun and adjective cf. 2.208-10.
258. Latonigenis: Diana and Phoebus were the children of Latona.
271. diem: as the glossators point out, this stands for *claritatem*, which must be that of the stars.
276. thiasos: *thyasi* are strictly associated with the worship of Bacchus, but here Joseph uses the word to denote festivities in general.
debile vulgus: not a very elegant way of describing the gentle sex. Another example of Joseph's anti-feminism.
282. facinus votumque: hendiadys for *facinorosum votum*.
283. Cf. Virg.*Aen*.8.712.
284. Paris is snatched: medieval anti-feminist views tended to blame Helen for the Trojan War. The example of Eve in the Old Testament was enthusiastically applied to all situations.
284f. The expression is full of irony.
287. firebrands: cf. 155n.
heu, perdite, nescis: cf. Virg.*Aen*.4.541.
289. Herculea corruptior unda: another allusive statement. The water in question is the marshwater of Lerna. It was not itself poisonous but the monster that lived in it, the hydra, was.
290. Bellorofonteo flagrantior igne: another similarly allusive remark. The fire in question was that of the Chimaera that Bellerophon was sent to kill.
fair weather: a pessimistic outlook on life or perhaps a prudent view of the English climate!

293. Lilibea vorago: Charybdis was a whirlpool in Sicily near the promontory of Lilybaeum. The source for the term is probably Ovid, *Met*.13.726.

294. Scylla: cf. 1.368n.
Libicus tenor: the Syrtes. These were quicksands off the coast of Libya.

297. first embraces: according to legend Paris and Helen did not consummate their love on board ship, but waited until they stopped at the island of Tenedos. Joseph appears to follow this version and then to enlarge upon it in his own inimitable fashion!
multa: strictly a fine, but here used as a synonym for *poena*. Joseph seems to be obsessed by the thought of retribution for sinning. Cf. 1.38 and 378.

300. silence in its ignorance: it may be that the abstract is being used here for the concrete, in which case *inscia..silentia* would stand for *inscii..silentes*, referring to the *armati..cives*.

304. deo: *Baccho* for *vino*.

310. violator of hospitality: as with 279 there is a suspicion that Joseph is alluding to the version of the story in which Paris was the guest of Menelaus and Helen. If so, he would be following in Ovid's footsteps, for in the *Met*. Ovid is not always consistent in the telling of the different legends.

311. nobile vulgus: irony again. At 315 it is *pauper*.

319. Paphie: cf. 2.293n.

322. homeland: according to some versions of the story she regretted her adultery.

324. imagined: Joseph actually says 'feigned', presumably wishing to paint as black a picture as possible of Helen, but he seems to lose consistency. See previous note.

325. Mide fluvios: the Hermus, Tagus and Pactolus were rivers said to contain gold. Legend attributed this to the fact that Midas had bathed in the Pactolus when everything he touched turned to gold. Cf. Ovid, *Met*.11.87, Hyginus 191, Vat.Myth.1.88, 2.117 and 3.10.8. Ovid, *Met*.2.251 says the Tagus contained gold. The Pactolus was a tributary of the Hermus. Joseph, or perhaps his source, seems to have associated them all with Midas or else he is simply using 'Midas' to mean 'gold'.

326. vellera Serum: *vellera* are strictly fleeces and thus refer to wool. Here Joseph stretches the meaning to 'silk'. The Seres were an eastern people usually thought to be the Chinese.

mundi maioris: see 2.596n.

326f. Cf. Ovid, *Met*.8.830ff.

330-33. This description of failed love-making, due to Paris' *ejaculatio praeceps* reveals the medieval way of thinking. Copulation with the woman on top was a sin for which penance was required by the church. Joseph blackens the image of Helen even more because despite being paid generously she does not actually succeed in making love to Paris. The glossators are clear on this point. Joseph appears to be subverting Virg.*Aen*.1.717ff. for his purpose.

332. Dione: I have translated by 'ardour'. The glossators are more explicit with '*scilicet spina*'.

339. news: that Paris is returning. Its position immediately following the love-scene is rather unfortunate. Dares 11.

347. Cf. Stat. *Theb*.10.842.

350. ordinary people: another slight on the *plebs*.

366-74. vengeance: Joseph's prophetess is madder than Virgil's (*Aen*.6.241ff.).

374ff. Cf. Ovid, *Her*.5.117-24.

378. Cf. Ovid, *Her*.7.139.

393. holy name: marriage.

394. phalerare: based on *phalerae* 'trappings'.
adultery: *incestus* was originally used for sexual relations with blood relatives or nuns. Its use became enlarged to cover cases that would normally be termed rape or adultery.

400. Europe: Joseph actually says 'lands given the name of Europa'. The ancients thought that the name of the continent originated from Europa, the daughter of Agenor, whom Jupiter seduced in the guise of a bull. Cf. Ovid, *Met*.2.830ff., and *Ecloga Theoduli* 144.

412f. Mt Malea etc: There were two mountains of this name. Here it is presumably the one on Lesbos that is meant as the other is in Sparta and would thus be inappropriate in the present circumstances. However, it is difficult to know which leaders Joseph might have in mind. Dares 11, followed by Joseph at 432, says Castor and Pollux were there, but they did not return to Sparta. Larissa suggests that Achilles is meant, but see 147n. The glossators are silent on these lines. Perhaps Joseph just means 'from all corners of Greece'?

417. poetic muses: according to the glossators it is Lucan and Statius that Joseph has in mind here.

421. The number of ships is found at Dares 14.

427ff. The drowning of Castor and Pollux is given at Dares 11. It is probably a fiction to explain why they did not take part in the Trojan War. However, both Dares and Joseph will include their portraits among those actually fighting.

429f. orbata..lustra: Joseph seems to have modified Virgil's image of *deserta ferarum/lustra* (Aen.3.646-47) and added the reference to the eagle (*fulminis ales*) with the famous prophecy of Merlin '*Catuli leonis in equoreos pisces transformabuntur et aquila eius super montem Aravium nidificabit* 'The cubs of the lion will be transformed into fishes of the sea and his eagle will nest upon Mt Aravium' (Geoffrey of Monmouth, *Historia Regum Britanniae*, 7.3) in mind. The use is appropriate as Merlin was supposed to be referring to the drowning of two sons of Henry I, the half-brothers William and Richard, in the White Ship disaster in 1120.

432. Lesbos: see 412n.

433. nil decoctius audet: Cf. Persius 1.125.

439. two-fold: *procella* is a storm that has wind and rain.

456f. fury: to be taken both literally, referring to the drowning of Castor and Pollux, and allegorically, being weighed down with one's sinfulness, as the glosses show.

458. those: like Empedocles, according to the glossators, citing Hor. *A.P.* 464-66, who jumped into Mt Etna in order to become immortal.

459. those onto the rocks: e.g. Castor and Pollux.

462. Joseph is here referring to the more common story of the Dioscuri as stars whose alternance in the sky reflects their shared mortality and immortality.

464. feralis: 'deadly' not 'bestial'. The glosses cite '*feron Grece, mors Latine*'. Cf. *Grecismus* p.38.150.

472f. The belief in the possible return of King Arthur was common in Joseph's time. While Joseph's scepticism of the supernatural is consistent with his belief that pagans were wrong-headed, these lines also show that he was loyal to the Plantagenets. The monks of Glastonbury were to discover Arthur's tomb, thus putting the myth of Arthur's return from Avallon to rest. Cf. Henry of Settimello 3.37-38 and Walter of Châtillon, *Alexandreis* 7.412. For a contrary view see Stephen of Rouen, *Draco Normannicus*. The topic is discussed by R.S. Loomis, *Arthurian Literature in the Middle Ages*, (Oxford, 1961) 64-67. As there is no gloss on these lines in P they may not have been present in the original version of the poem (see Introd. p.6).